11/05

D0604986

DEMOCRACY AND POPULISM

JOHN LUKACS

Democracy and Populism

Fear & Hatred

Yale University Press   NEW HAVEN & LONDON

Designed by James J. Johnson and set in Minion types by Integrated Publishing Solutions

Printed in the United States of America by R.R. Donnelley & Sons

Library of Congress Cataloging-in-Publication Data

Lukacs, John, 1924–

 Democracy and populism : fear and hatred / John Lukacs

  p. cm.

 Includes index

 ISBN 0-300-10773-0 (alk. paper)

  1. Political science—United States—History—20th century. 2. United States—Politics and government—20th century. 3. Ideology—United States—History—20th century. I. Title.

JA84.U5L85 2005

320.5′0973′0904—dc22   2004058450

A catalogue record for this book is available from the British Library.

The paper in this book meets the guidelines for permanence and durability of the Committee on Production Guidelines for Book Longevity of the Council on Library Resources.

10 9 8 7 6 5 4 3 2 1

Contents

Preface

Tocqueville one hundred and seventy years ago: "A new science of politics is necessary for a new world." It has not been forthcoming.

This admittedly radical (here and there) and general historical essay has one large limitation. Its material is limited to the United States, the English-speaking world, and Europe. Its arguments, its evidences and illustrations, are drawn only from this portion of the world, inhabited mostly by the white race, the extent and the numbers of which are now declining. This limitation accords with the limits of my knowledge and of my interests. At this time of so many vacuous generalizations by so many intellectuals who know less and less about more and more (the obverse of the, often fatuous, nineteenth-century quip about specialists who know more and more about less and less), I think that my geographic and cultural restrictions for the theme and scope of this book may be especially proper. For this work attempts descriptions and diagnoses not of material but of mental conditions and tendencies, in accord with my belief that in this mass democratic age material conditions, almost always, matter less than mental conditions and inclinations—indeed, that the very material order (or disorder) of the world is not at all the fundament but the consequence of what many people think. And about the thinking and the mental structures and the traditional (or modern) psychic inclinations of my fellow human beings beyond the (admittedly imprecise) boundaries of what remains of Western civilization I know little or nothing.

A few passages of this book, often rewritten, were taken from a few previously published writings of mine.

1

{TOCQUEVILLE'S VISION OF HISTORY}

ALEXIS DE TOCQUEVILLE was a visionary, and a historical, even more than a political, thinker. He finished and published the first volume of his *Democracy in America* one hundred and seventy years ago. Note the honest precision of his title: *De la démocratie en Amérique:* "About democracy in America." His theme was democracy, as it then existed in America. His first volume was mainly about America, his second volume, published five years later, mainly about democracy. For us this second volume is even more relevant and timely than the first. His contemporaries did not think so; that second volume was criticized, wrongly so; the first volume was not.

Of course much has happened since. America is not what it was then. The American people are not what they were then. America is no longer the only, the main, prototype of democracy in the world. Perhaps Tocqueville should be reversed. For a book remains to be written, with the title

and theme of *American Democracy*: that is, what is particularly American in the political and social conditions of the
United States; what and how do they differ from French
or British or German or Japanese or Russian or Ruritarian
democracy—now, when all around us, all across the globe
seethes, bubbles, froths the still spreading tide, the democratization of the world?

Tocqueville proposed this question already at the end of
his first volume:

> Those who, after having read this book, should
> imagine that my intention in writing it was to pro-
> pose the laws and customs of the Anglo-Americans
> for the imitation of all democratic communities
> would make a great mistake; they must have paid
> more attention to the form than to the substance of
> my thought. My aim has been to show, by the ex-
> ample of America, that laws, and especially customs,
> may allow a democratic people to remain free. But I
> am very far from thinking that we ought to follow
> the example of the American democracy and copy
> the means that it has employed to attain this end;
> for I am well aware of the influence which the na-
> ture of a country and its political antecedents exer-
> cise upon its political constitution; and I should
> regard it as a great misfortune for mankind if lib-
> erty were to exist all over the world under the same
> features.

And yet: the evolving history of the democratization of the world is well-nigh inseparable from the Americanization of the world. Not identical; but inseparable. "To make the world safe for democracy": this hapless idea of an American president, Wilson (a southern New Englander; a Virginian Puritan), remained more enduring than the revolutionary ideas of his contemporary—they died but a few days apart—the (partly Tartar, partly German) goateed demagogue Lenin. Perhaps Wilson's mindless phrase ought to be—may still be—reversed too: "how to make democracy safe for the world," which *is* a big question that Tocqueville would have instantly understood.

Tocqueville is not outdated, since many of the questions that he stated, or suggested, have become more and more obvious. Is democracy the rule of the people, or, more precisely: rule by the people? No: because it is, really and actually, rule in the name of the people. That is not simpler but more complicated than anything before. Yes: in its predominant sense democracy is the rule of the majority. (And how is this majority composed, formed, what does it consist of?) Here liberalism enters. (It did not, and does not always.) Majority rule is tempered by the legal assurance of the rights of minorities, and of individual men and women. And when this temperance is weak, or unenforced, or unpopular, then democracy is nothing more (or else) than populism. More precisely: then it is nationalist populism.

Neither "nationalism" nor "populism"—*nationalisme* or *populisme*—were terms used by Tocqueville. He understood such phenomena: but these words did not even exist in the French language during his lifetime.

But exist they do; and our question is how traditional democracy can exist much longer, when traditional liberalism has decayed. Tocqueville did not have to face this; but we do. And as we get there—again, more precisely: how did we get here?—we must look at something greater, which was Tocqueville's vision. This was the change from the aristocratic to the democratic age in the history of mankind. A vision grand and simple. So often it has been inadequately recognized, a classic case of not seeing a forest for the trees. (Perhaps George Orwell's twentieth-century statement fits appropriately here: "We have now sunk to a depth where the restatement of the obvious is the duty of intelligent men.")

Tocqueville was a historian as much as a political theorist or a sociologist. (Unlike Spengler or Toynbee or others he had not, he cared not for a philosophy of history. The contrary was true: his philosophy was historical.) Of course he knew a fair amount of history; of course he knew the customary categories, Ancient, Middle, Modern. Different ages of history meant much to him, including the changing conditions of human existence and, perhaps especially, of thinking (something that—so-called—postmodern historians have lately been grappling with, the history of mentalities, *mentalités:* as Oscar Wilde would put it, pursuing the obvious with the enthusiasm of short-sighted detectives). Tocqueville, like his close predecessor Burke (with whom, however, he did not always agree), understood the inevitable historicity of human existence. He saw something even simpler and greater, which was the division of history into something else than chronological periods: the Aristocratic, and the Democratic Age. The first was receding during his lifetime, the second rising and growing, though not yet universal. Since Adam and Eve people were ruled by minorities. Now no longer. He understood what this meant, with all of the humility of a Christian. "I cannot believe," he once wrote, "that God has for several centuries been pushing two or three hundred million men toward equality just to make them wind up under a Tiberian or Claudian despotism. Verily, that wouldn't be worth the trouble. Why He is drawing us toward democracy, I do not know; but embarked on a vessel that I did not build, I am at least trying to use it to gain the nearest port." He also understood that this was a gradual development. But we live more than a century and a half after him. He did not (how could he?) foresee the ending of the Modern Age, in the midst of which we now are. He did see that what was happening was the decline of aristocracy and the rise of democracy—sometimes rapidly, sometimes slowly, sometimes simultaneously, sometimes not, sometimes more politically than socially, sometimes less so.

From us, from our perspective, this is now largely over. (Perspective is an inevitable component of reality; and all perspective is, at least to some extent, historical, just as all knowledge depends on memory.) We can see—more: we *ought* to see—that the entire so-called Modern Age, 1500–

2000, especially and particularly in the West, was marked by this dual development: aristocracy retreating, democracy advancing: and that this was once something new, and that this is now at an end.

{THE ENDING OF "MIXED" GOVERNMENT}

MONARCHY, ARISTOCRACY, DEMOCRACY: these forms of government, these social conditions, have come to resemble their origins in the past only superficially. These categories and their definitions are Greek. But there is a great mistake to think that Athenian democracy or Spartan aristocracy or Lycurgian monarchy—or, at that, "government" in Greece, or "family" in Rome—had much, if anything, in common with our acquaintance, our experience, our usage of these terms.

At the same time we can recognize, and respect, the knowledge and the understanding of these classical models by our predecessors, champions and architects of our liberties. Their acquaintance with ancient history was the source of the respect they had for what they, especially in the seventeenth and eighteenth centuries, invoked as Mixed Government. They had read (or at least pretended to have read) their Aristotle. But perhaps even more important was their knowledge and understanding of perennial human nature, a capacity that has been compromised, overlaid, diluted, and perhaps even largely lost now. In any event: they knew that no form of human government can be perfect because human nature was imperfect. Hence their advocacies for the—relatively—best governments for civilized states were those that combined monarchical and aristocratic and democratic elements. That was an achievement of Western civilization. Entire constitutions rose from it: constitutional monarchy in England, the Constitution of the United States, the original (and then rapidly destroyed) impulse of at least some of the French reformers before and in 1789. I need not describe this further: this book is not a treatise in the history of political science.

Still it is interesting to contemplate how and why the framers of the American Constitution chose to begin its text with a bang: "We the People . . ."* After all, they, too, had their doubts about that inchoate term: "The People." In any event: what every high school student knows or, rather, ought to know, is that the Constitution encompassed, at least originally, the ideals of Mixed Government: a "monarchical" element represented by a president and his powers;

---

*The original version began: "The people of . . . ," enumerating the thirteen states. However, Rhode Island and New York were not willing to sign. So Gouverneur Morris rephrased this to "We the People . . . ," something vaguer, less binding, more acceptable. (This from a man who once called "the people" "reptiles." He was no populist.)

an "aristocratic" element by the electoral college and by the restrictions, nominations, elections of senators and of the Senate (and somewhat later by the Supreme Court); the "democratic" element by the House of Representatives.

It does not require much historical knowledge (though it may require a certain historical perspective) to see that many, if not all, of the "aristocratic" elements of the Constitution (as also in other countries) have gradually disappeared or were washed away during the past two hundred years, while the monarchic powers of the presidency and the democratic extent of majority rule became more and more overwhelming. (We ought to recognize, too, how the American Constitution, with all its vaunted unique achievements, collapsed in 1861. After more than a decade of pulling and tugging, it was evidently incapable of preventing the break-up of the republic and of a civil war.)

Tocqueville wrote little about mixed government, or about what Americans still call "checks and balances." But he believed in the few benefits of remaining nondemocratic institutions, restraining total and untrammeled democracy. Thus, for example, in *Democracy in America,* he observed and praised the American judiciary system and American lawyers (he called them "légistes," not "avocats"), suggesting that they represented a sort of American elite, with the principal role of restraining unlimited majority rule and the potential tyranny of the latter. Thus, for example, Tocqueville respected the England of his times (except for its practices

in Ireland), including the presence of certain British aristocrats in politics,* as befits a constitutional monarchy. But a
century and a half later we need not waste much thought on
what happened with American lawyers† or with the British
aristocracy. The political and the social functions that Tocqueville saw and ascribed to them are gone. Democracy has become unlimited, untrammeled, universal.

It is worth noticing that monarchies still exist. (Exist, rather
than prevail.) Constitutional monarchies, all of them, which
is to the good: but we must understand, too, that they exist
only on popular sufferance: democracy and majority rule
may put an end to them in an instant. Still, the relationship
of monarchy and democracy, different as it has been from
the relationship of aristocracy and democracy, deserves a
rapid cursory look. A hereditary monarchy lends a certain

---

*Winston Churchill in 1909, when he had become a Liberal, quoted
the recent words of Lord Curzon: "All civilisation has been the work of aristocracies." Churchill: "Why, it would be much more true to say that the
upkeep of the aristocracy has been the hard work of all civilisations"—
funny and telling, both more and less than a demagogic witticism.

†Luke 11:52–54: "Woe to your lawyers, for you have taken away the
key to knowledge: you yourselves have not entered in, you have hin-
dered. And as he [Jesus] was saying these things to them, the Pharisees
and the lawyers began violently to urge him, and to stop his mouth
about many things. Lying in wait for him, and seeking to catch something from his mouth, that they might accuse him."

sense of stability to a democratic people, the sense of a family (something that may have emerged as late as during Victoria's reign in Britain). That is not so under the rule of an elective monarchy such as the American one (even though during the last one hundred years popular interest in the American presidents' wives or families has not decreased but increased). Even more important: at moments of grave national crises a hereditary monarch—whatever his other weaknesses or shortcomings—may save an entire country from destruction. In 1943 it was the king of Italy (Victor Emmanuel III) who had Mussolini arrested and deposed; in 1945 it was the emperor (Hirohito) who declared Japan's surrender, the impact of which was even more decisive than either the two atomic bombs cast on Japan or Stalin's declaration of war a week before. In 1989 and afterward the United States may have been mistaken for not favoring the return of constitutional monarchies in Romania and Yugoslavia and even in Afghanistan. But then in 1917 and 1918 many Americans, and especially liberal and Progressive political spokesmen and intellectuals, argued that World War I, "the war to end all wars," was a war between Democracy, incarnated by the United States, against Monarchy, incarnated by the Kaiser's Germany (conveniently overlooking a number of monarchies on the Allied side).

Still: even if constitutional and hereditary monarchies can, and perhaps even should, coexist with a democratic society and state, their continued existence does not vitiate the overall condition, the unchallenged principle of popular sovereignty, worldwide.

❦

The coexistence—more, a mutual dependence—of monarchy and democracy long preceded the American and the French (and even the English) revolutions. In the beginning of the Modern Age the emerging bourgeois classes sought, and applauded, the rising powers of kings, protecting them from the ravages of aristocracies. Tocqueville was among the first to notice that in France the administrative centralization of the state began well during the near-absolute monarchy and then remained predominant and unchallenged during and after the French Revolution. He thought and wrote that centralization, meaning the ever extending power of central governmental administration, could be endemic for democracy, including the prospects of an eventual welfare state. His prophetic concern with this is well known. He also understood the particular vices and shortcomings of his own French aristocracy in this regard—this was his main criticism of Edmund Burke, who, in Tocqueville's view, was right about the excesses and the dangers of the French Revolution, but wrong in his illusions of the benefices and order of the aristocratic-monarchical order that had preceded it. Anyhow, besides the failures of the aristocracy, a compulsive inclination to categorical governmental regulations was particularly French, one outcome of a geometrical spirit that was Cartesian (and not Pascalian). Beyond France we may note another important inclination: the bourgeois's dependence on the protection of their monarchs included an impulse that was, and remains, typical of the bourgeoisie and of liberals: an element of fear.

Were anyone to write a classic work on the history of democracy (which of course is not identical with the history of freedom, a grand and enormous topic with which Lord Acton tried, in vain, to grapple), he must begin neither with Greece more than two thousand nor with America and France more than two hundred years ago. He must consider England, because of radical and democratic beliefs and customs current among its people—and because of the migration of English and Scots people and of their ideas back and forth across the Atlantic in the seventeenth century. And even earlier, of course—I am referring not to popular revolts in the English Middle Ages or some of the Protestant radical reformers, but to an aristocratic thinker such as Lord Henry Savile, who as early as in 1580 wrote (but of course did nothing about it): "Democratia est optimus status reipublicae." And even under the most baneful and darkest skies of the English Civil War we may glimpse the already extant bright sparks of English liberties. There it is, in 1648, Lady Fairfax shouting her defiance of the government and of the king's trial from the gallery of the Painted Chamber, shocking people but remaining unpunished for the bravery of her convictions; there is more than occasional fairness in some of the newspapers as they suggest their defense of the monarchy; there are soldiers and parliamentary commissioners expressing their reluctance of the king's condemnation; there is that very last public speech of the condemned Charles. All this in the mid-seventeenth century, at the time of a then swiftly descending military dictatorship. Nothing like this in France after 1789, not to speak of life under modern dictators. Napoleon did not understand this. In St. Helena he mused that had he invaded England in 1803, "I would have proclaimed a republic . . . the abolition of the nobility and of the house of peers . . . liberty, equality, and the sovereignty of the people . . . democracy." (One hundred and twenty years later Hitler's ideas would not have been very different.)

Any history of modern democracy (which, I again insist, is not at all identical with any history of "liberty") must consider the peoples of northwestern Europe, Scandinavia and Holland, well before the "Enlightenment." The Dutch rebels who did not recognize Philip II proclaimed their "republic." In Sweden the struggle between the "Hats" and "Caps" in the eighteenth century was one between the aristocracy and the bourgeois, not yet involving the lowest classes— among a people whose categorical respect for moderation and compromise appeared only later. Some of the Swedish political leaders admired English democracy. As early as the late seventeenth century there were four estates in Sweden, the fourth the peasants. So the eventually deep and enduring democratic order of that country and people had not only deep roots but was beginning to be institutionalized long ago. And then in Scandinavia, too—as also in the Netherlands, after the great troubles of the Dutch during the French revolutionary period, the coexistence with—indeed, the mutual dependence of—the middle and lower classes on a constitutional monarchy were, and largely remain, remarkable.

But meanwhile the principle of popular sovereignty was slowly, gradually, becoming universal.* Wherefore I must conclude this cursory run through some of the earlier histories of modern democracy, and of the ancient virtues and the early modern examples of Mixed Government. We must open our tired eyes. Mixed government has now become a thing of the past. It cannot be restored. Aristocracy is gone (even socially: the respect and the, often snobbish, admiration for it that still prevailed not so long ago). Probably, given human nature, brutal ruling classes will arise, coming to the fore, governing many nations in the future, I fear. After that, again, many people, oppressed by fear, may seek protection from a single ruler. Enough of this: this writer is

---

*A recent virtuous contrary voice. A West German democratic constitution was being drafted after 1946. Heinz Krekeler, a member of Parliament and of a constitutional commission, opposed the fundamental sentence: "All power derives from the people." "I succeeded," he wrote, "with a simple argument that my colleagues found very convincing. The making of popular sovereignty absolute—interestingly, only the Communist faction wanted it—means that the sovereign people may then again dispose of democracy and introduce a dictatorship. There must be something that limits popular sovereignty, and these are the basic values and basic rights of [our constitution]."

no prophet. Sufficient it is to see that the principle of popular sovereignty is now universal; to see what its politics have become, what they consist of, and what are its prime and principal dangers.

{"RIGHT" AND "LEFT":
THEIR CONSERVATIVE MISREADINGS}

O NE HUNDRED AND SEVENTY YEARS AGO Tocqueville remarked: "A new science of politics is necessary for a new world."

It has not been forthcoming.

Two terms, "Right" and "Left," came to be applied to politics and to ideas during, and here and there even before, his lifetime. He used them seldom, if at all: but there they were. The French Revolution (and thereafter the seating of deputies in national assemblies and parliaments) led to their general employment, in many languages. Yet these two terms could have been applicable to political and other realities well before 1789. John Adams was a "Rightist." Samuel Adams a "Leftist." The English Puritans were "Leftists." The English Royalists were "Rightists." Protestants were, by and large, "Leftists," Roman Catholics "Rightists." Marius was "Left-

ist," Sulla "Rightist"—we may as well go back to Cain and
Abel. None of these designations is precise, and every one of
them is at least to some extent arguable. As always, Samuel
Johnson is right: "Definitions are tricks for pedants." Still,
Right and Left retain *some* meaning, even now.

Yet not much. For at least one hundred years after the
American and the French revolutions there *was* a fundamental difference. The "Right," by and large, feared and rejected the principle of popular sovereignty. The "Left" advocated or supported or at least would propose democracy.
It still does. The "Right," for a long time, was not populist.
But now often it is—which is perhaps a main argument of
this book.

The French Revolution had opponents—serious opponents and critics—from its beginning. As it went on there
were many more critics who were appalled by its excesses.
But that the French Revolution was more good than bad
was, and remained, an unquestionable article of faith of all
believers in "Progress," ranging from liberals to Communists, for at least one hundred and fifty years after 1789. Russian Communists in 1917 sang the "Marseillaise" and then
named one of their battleships "Marat"; history professors
at Harvard, some of them the offspring of proper Boston
merchants, with gray ice on their faces, wrote books as late
as in the 1930s defending the bloody French Committee of
Public Safety. In 1889 the British ambassador to France refused to attend the ceremonies commemorating the one
hundredth anniversary of 1789. Fifty years later, on the Four-

teenth of July in 1939, French and British dignitaries relished the sight of French and British regiments marching down together on the Champs-Elysées. Less than a year later they would be broken into smithereens by a German army, vitalized, inspired, equipped by the populist Hitler.

Then, during the last fifty or sixty years, there came a slight but significant perceptual change. There came—*pace* Burke and following Burke—a novel historical appreciation of the differences between the American and the French revolutions. A few thinkers rediscovered Burke, the Burke who had some sympathy for the cause of the American revolutionaries but none for the French ones. This intellectual response had much to do with the Second World War. The proof of the pudding was in the eating, after all. France had collapsed in 1940 while the United States went on triumphantly, to rule much of the world. After 1789, perhaps even because of 1789, France went on the decline. After *their* 1789 (the actual launching of the United States) Americans and their democratic republic went from triumph to triumph. Not that American democracy was "Rightist" and French republicanism "Leftist": but there was a moral in their historical record. Then, a few years after 1945—during the so-called Cold War—a few more small nails were hammered into the coffin of the French Revolution's once so shining reputation. The word "totalitarianism" now covered both extremes, Hitler and Stalin, the "extreme" Right and the "extreme" Left; and had not some of the ideas and many of the practices of the French revolutionaries, at least after

1792, been early examples, even prototypes, of a Totalitarian Democracy? (This was the title and the theme of a political thinker, Jacob Talmon, then in Israel.) Meanwhile in France, too, though well after 1945, historians rediscovered Tocqueville, at long last. Among them François Furet, an erstwhile Communist, who argued that, yes, there was a constant strife in France between partisans and adversaries of the Revolution and about the principles of 1789; but by 1880 the republican principles were accepted and the French ship of state was no longer menaced by a great division among the crew—a thesis with some substance but not much. By the end of the twentieth century even ubiquitous and publicly celebrated liberal historians such as Simon Schama wrote about the French Revolution having been both Good and Bad, with emphatic descriptions of dramatic scenes and personae representing the latter. All of this was part and parcel of a wider and deeper intellectual development. Two hundred years after 1789—let us face it—the French Revolution had become boring.

"Part and parcel" because—again, let us face it—somehow much of the entire (and so largely French) Enlightenment had become boring. Or at least irrelevant: because of its mechanical and rationalist philosophy of human nature.

But here we come to the mistaken view that many conservatives adopted during the twentieth century and that they have even now. This is that the rise of nationalist antiliberalism meant a great historical reaction against 1789. In 1933 and 1934 the then-leading German conservative,

Franz von Papen, said that what was happening in Germany in 1933 was *the* great answer of history against the, largely French-inspired, ideas of 1789. (And this is the enduring mistake of many conservatives, who despise the "Left" more than they distance themselves from "extremists" on the "Right.") But Hitler was someone very different from a counterrevolutionary; and the German 1933 was not a counterrevolutionary movement. Nothing was further from Hitler (or even from Mussolini, or from Perón, etc., etc.) than to see anything good in monarchy or aristocracy (let alone in the world of the eighteenth century). He was a populist; and a revolutionary; and, at least in some ways, a democrat. Evidences of this, in his words and acts, could fill a small book.

We shall—alas, inevitably—return to Hitler later in these pages; but it is here that his example was, and remains, proof that the ancient categories "Right" and "Left" have become, at least in one important sense, outdated. Where to put him? Was Hitler to the "Right" or to the "Left" of Churchill? Was he more "Rightist" than the pope? Was he more, or less, "reactionary" than, say, Franco? It is not only that Hitler or Mussolini or Perón (or even Stalin) were professed populists; it is, too, that most twentieth-century dictatorships and/or "the tyranny of the majority" were neither reactionary nor conservative. Two hundred years after 1789 "Right" and "Left" still retain some meaning, but less and less. And much of the same applies to their once offsprings, conservatives and liberals. For, if conservatives have a fatal inclination to accept populists and extreme nationalists for their allies on the "Right," the liberals' misreading of the latter is as bad, if not worse.

{A LIBERAL MISREADING}

UCH A MISREADING OF HISTORY—or, in its author's words, of "A Chapter in the History of Ideas"—is evident, for example, in a celebrated essay by a celebrated thinker, in Isaiah Berlin's "Joseph de Maistre and the Origins of Fascism."* It calls for a brief examination, since it is replete with the—alas, still enduring—myopia of liberals about history, indeed about human nature.

Joseph de Maistre was an adversary of the French Revolution and of its ideas; and of democracy as well as of liberal abstractions of humanity. He was a clear writer, while not an altogether attractive person, with his sense of being a Demosthenes largely unheard, and also with a touch of a somewhat frustrated parvenu, unnoticed by the very people whose cause he so eloquently defended. He *was* radically re-

---

*Isaiah Berlin, *The Crooked Timber of Humanity: Chapters in the History of Ideas* (New York, 1991).

actionary, and not merely conservative. His views of mankind and of government were certainly closer to those of Hobbes than to those of Locke (or those of Bossuet rather than of Montesquieu). Maistre's perception and analysis of the French Revolution had a few similarities with those of Burke; but their views of human nature differed considerably, indeed deeply. "The people," Burke once said, "must never be regarded as incurable." Maistre would never agree to that. He believed, as Berlin cites him, that men can be saved only "by authority. They must be reminded at every instant of their lives of the frightening mystery that lies at the heart of creation; they must be purged by perpetual suffering, must be humbled by being made conscious of their stupidity, malice, and helplessness." According to Berlin, this deep pessimism about human nature is "the heart of totalitarianisms, of both left and right, of our terrible century." "Maistre may have spoken the language of the past, but the content of what he had to say presages the future . . . of the great counterrevolutionary movement that culminated in Fascism."

But the very opposite is true. Maistre *was* a reactionary, a man of "the extreme Right"; Hitler and Mussolini, and Perón, etc., were not. They were *not* deeply pessimistic about human nature. (Hitler, for one, was an idealist not a materialist: an idealist of a dreadfully German and frightfully deterministic variety, and a believer in the power of ideas over matter.) These men knew how to appeal to the masses— something that would have filled Maistre with horror. They knew (as did Proudhon but not Marx) that people are moved by (and at times even worship) evidences of power, rather than by propositions of social contracts. It was not so much Joseph de Maistre as it was Gustave Flaubert who illuminated this with a small bright flash. Sénécal is a figure in Flaubert's *Sentimental Education* who presaged the twentieth century. Sénécal is one of a group of sentimental young liberals and radicals before the French revolution of 1848 (which was a hobbling repetition of 1789), but then he turns up as a brutal police official in the dictatorial regime of Louis Napoleon.* *He,* Sénécal, was "a forerunner of Fascism," not Joseph Maistre. (Oh well . . . the eye of a great novelist may penetrate deeper than the cerebrations of so many political thinkers.)

Isaiah Berlin writes of "the influence of Jesuit ideas" on Maistre—a tired recurrence of old suspicious Liberal ideas, as also what Berlin attributes to Maistre: "Faith is truly faith only when it is blind; once it looks for justification it is done for." (No: true faith, like true love, is never "blind": Pascal.) According to Berlin, Maistre was Jesuitical and hopelessly backward, opposed to science. "The very language of science to De Maistre is something degraded; and he notes, prophetically enough, that the degradation of language is always the surest sign of the degradation of a people." Well, in this Maistre was quite right; indeed, this concern with

---

*Who was elected by universal manhood suffrage by the majority of the French people.

language is at least similar to that of a very different man one hundred and fifty years later, of George Orwell. But now consider that Hitler, like Mussolini and others, had nothing against science and technology; rather the contrary, he believed in its benefits for "the people."

In sum, Joseph de Maistre, unlike modern dictators, loathed the idea of popular sovereignty; as Berlin cites him, "a principle so dangerous that even if it were true, it would be necessary to conceal it." This was exactly what the modern dictators had *not* done; instead of concealing it they appealed to it. Maistre was a true counterrevolutionary, a man of the Extreme Old Right—which none of the dictators of the twentieth century was, not even Franco. It would have been better if they had been that—but such a speculation is both unrealistic and unhistorical—as is the protracted application of "Right" and "Left," and of their "extremes," along a linear or even a hemicyclic design or model.

{CONSERVATIVES AND LIBERALS}

THESE TWO DESIGNATIONS, "conservative" and "liberal," were first applied to political parties in England during the 1820s. They were successors to, and substitutions for, the previous categories Tory and Whig, particularly English as these had been. (Edmund Burke, whom, for many reasons, we can see as a founding father of modern "conservatism," was a Whig.) "Liberal," surely in English (but also in a few other western European languages), was an approbatory adjective long before its political employment. Its meaning encompassed many matters. "Liberal" meant civilized, open-hearted (perhaps even more than broad-minded), "free" and "generous": so it was used by Jane Austen but also by other Englishmen and Englishwomen before her time. Occasionally "liberal" meant the opposite of "servile" and "mechanical," especially in the eighteenth century. (On rare occasions it could mean "licentious," a usage that disappeared after the seventeenth century.) "Conservative" had a less spacious meaning and etymological history; it meant conserving or preserving; it was rarely used as a political designation until the early nineteenth century.

After 1820, then, the conservative vs. liberal dichotomy, or debate, or dialogue, became continental European as well as English. (It is interesting that the ascription of certain Whigs and reformers as "liberals" actually came to England from Spain, where the "liberales" were those who opposed the autocratic monarchy of Ferdinand VII at Cádiz in 1820.) Whatever its verbal origins, the Conservative vs. Liberal configuration dominated British as well as European politics during most of the nineteenth century, in some countries for some time even thereafter.

This was not so in the United States. There was no Tory party here. Federalists and Democratic-Republicans; Whigs and Democrats; Republicans and Democrats—all of them eschewed the "conservative" designation, for more than one hundred and sixty years. At times some of them were—relatively—more conservative than were others; but for a long time none of them wished to acquire the questionable reputation of being called "conservative." The only exceptions were a few political publicists in the South in the 1850s, to whom not many people, even in the South, paid much attention. For in the states of the American South, too, the few self-styled conservatives were proponents of popular sovereignty. (The concordance and collusion of American conservatism and American populism deserves another book by itself.) Democracy, and popular sovereignty, had become the sacrosanct American principle and political reality, latest by the 1820s; and so they are today.

And yet—in the 1950s there came a change. Since then, "liberal" began to lose its shine and appeal; soon it even acquired a negative popular reputation—while "conservative" became to connote many things (though not necessarily conserving or preserving).*

Tocqueville, who saw the two adjectives emerge and rapidly become near-universal, was not altogether pleased with their accuracy. On occasion he would say or write that he was conservative in some things, liberal in others; on other occasions he would write that he did not really belong to either category; yet at other times he said that he was not comfortable with being seen as between them. (For us it may be sufficient to observe that while during their lifetime, and for a long time thereafter, both Burke and Tocqueville

*We may pinpoint the beginning of this change rather exactly. As late as 1950 Senator Robert A. Taft, idol of almost all present American conservatives, felt compelled to say that he was not a conservative but an "old-fashioned liberal." As late as 1951 the demagogue Joseph McCarthy (alas, another idol of at least some American conservatives) still used "liberal" as a positive adjective at least once. In his speech on 14 June 1951, accusing General Marshall, he said that the latter, along with Dean Acheson, was part of "a conspiracy so immense as to dwarf any previous such venture in the history of man. A conspiracy of infamy so black that, when it is finally exposed, the principles shall be forever deserving of the maledictions of all liberal men." By 1960 President Eisenhower, that supreme political opportunist, used the "conservative" designation as an approbatory and positive one.

were designated as "liberals" or, at most, as "conservative liberals," we—and others of the twentieth and twenty-first centuries—incline to see them as conservatives rather than liberals; or at least as liberal conservatives.)

In any event: those who muttered—and, on occasion, eloquently spoke—against the principle of popular sovereignty, against what Tocqueville called "the tyranny of the majority," were a scattering of serious thinkers in the United States, and more such in England and in Europe, where "democracy" was refused by conservatives, at least for awhile. And, at least during that golden age of politicophilosophical debates, from about 1820 to 1870, many liberals, too, were uneasy about democracy. They did not reject it entirely, but they tried their best to ascertain and to circumscribe its limits. They were aware, as was Tocqueville (though they seldom gave him enough credit) that Liberty and Equality were not identical, that their aspirations were not necessarily parallel, that they could be opposites on more than one occasion; and that insistence on one at the expense of the other could be disastrous. But after 1870 the practice (or at least the evocation) of democracy was, willy-nilly, adopted by almost all liberals, as well as by many conservatives. The clearest example was in Britain, where not only the Liberal but also the Conservative Party extended suffrage in a series of acts, from 1832 to 1867. When Lord Randolph Churchill spoke of "Tory Democracy" in the 1880s, this was more than demagoguery, it was a matter of historic perspective, a conviction.

Some time after 1870 began a great change. Its main

element was the—sometimes reluctant, but no matter—
acceptance of popular sovereignty by most liberals and by a
growing number of conservatives. A result of this was that
some of the principal differences between the two camps
began to fade. They did not disappear entirely—which is
why the two adjectives still retain some of their political and
philosophical and ideological meaning. Conservatives were
more attached to religion, monarchy, classes, traditions,
land; liberals to reason, parliamentarism (if not republicanism), free speech, commerce and trade, industry, "Progress."
And beneath and beside these categories their very lives
have become more and more alike. Conservatives aspired to
their seats in parliaments, to the comforts and pleasures of
living in the great cities of their countries and of the world;
they were beginning to be comfortable with Progress itself.
Liberals aspired to be respected and entitled by their monarchs and by high society at large; besides Progress they
began to appreciate political stability. During this last great
period of the coexistence of aristocracy and democracy
(more precisely: during the still extant social preeminence
of aristocracy together with the rise of political democracy),
the sharp colors and contrasts of the great conservative-
liberal debate were fading. This was not yet the case always
and everywhere: bitter conflicts and clashes between conservative and liberal politics and their advocates would still
occur in many places. But the time of their great dialogue,
especially in Europe, was largely over. There were more people

who sensed this than knew it then; we can see it, in retrospect, now.

Hegelians, Marxists, Darwinists, Freudians did not; most
of them still don't. Hegel died well before 1870, but his
scheme, or vision of history, lived on. He understood (like
most Germans) not only that ideas matter but that they
have consequences—even in the age of full-blown materialism which he had not yet lived to see. He also understood
that human history did not move like a pendulum, that ac-
tions and reactions of ideas—indeed, historical movements—
did not quite follow the laws of physics. That recognition
was correct; but his conclusions were not. According to his
well-known dialectic, Thesis was succeeded by Antithesis,
and then from the eventual struggle and confluence of the
two a Synthesis was bound to come. But that scheme was
too intellectual, idealistic as well as mechanical. The emerging confluence between conservatism and liberalism did
not result in a synthesis, except here and there, on certain
levels that did not matter much, especially not in the long
run. What came after 1870 was the emergence and the powerful attraction of two new enormous movements, nationalism and socialism, that turned out to rule most of the history of the twentieth century—indeed, most of the world
even now. They were not "syntheses": they were something
else. And of these two nationalism proved to be the most
powerful and enduring.

{POPULAR SOVEREIGNTY AND SOCIALISM}

T HE RISE AND HISTORY OF SOCIALISM is the easier of the two to sum up. It was a natural and expectable phenomenon, well before 1870. It represented—more, it was—a stage of evolution, of social change, of "progress." Whatever the pious (perhaps even more pious than hypo-critical) evocations of "le peuple" during the French, or even of "The People" during and after the American, for at least a century after each revolution the victorious people were the middle, rather than the lower classes. Attempts by radical revolutionaries, appealing to the lower classes, failed in France as well as in the United States (whether by Babeuf or by Shays's Rebellion, and in England as late as in 1848 by the Chartists). But could there be any doubt that at the full tide of materialism, of increasingly mobile and fluid soci-eties, of a vast increase of literacy, etc., etc., spokesmen of the so-called working classes would arise, demanding their share of government and of wealth? Much of this began before 1870. That rule by aristocracies would be followed by that of the middle classes, which then would be followed by that of the working class, constituting the majority, the people—this corresponded, at least largely, to Marx's dogmatic se-quence: Feudalism progressing into Capitalism and then

advancing to Socialism. Two attempts to hasten such a development by spokesmen of the working class, debouching
into bloody insurrections, occurred in France already in
June 1848 and in the spring of 1871, but they were defeated
by the national army, supported by the bourgeois. Yet this
did not mean that socialism was conquered, surely not in
the long run. Democracy kept advancing; and democracy
without the continuous rise and inclusion of the working
classes was an impossibility. That this political and social
progress of the lower classes could be furthered without
revolution was one of the achievements of the Western
world after 1870. Political socialism was beginning to divide
thereafter, into Social Democrats and the minority of radical revolutionaries who then became, sooner or later, Communists. This split between evolutionists and revolutionists
did not become definite until after 1918, but that was not
world-shaking, since Communists had gained power only
in Russia, which was a different world. Much more important was the circumstance that the earlier aspirations and
propositions and demands of socialists were—in retrospect,
almost inevitably—adopted and proposed by liberals and
even by conservatives. That was the expectable and un-
avoidable consequence of democracy, including universal
suffrage, universal literacy (of sorts), popular sovereignty.
In many places (though not everywhere) former liberals
and their descendants, more and more after 1870, concluded
that they needed the support of the lower classes, and not
only their votes: that the liberal and even some socialist

ideas and practices of social reforms and other enlightened ideas were, rather inevitably, part and parcel of the idea of "Progress." But conservatives, too—some of them even earlier in the nineteenth century—stirred, among other things, by their visceral and even moral dislike of the materialism and moneyed rule of the bourgeois and capitalists, would in some places and on many occasions put forward socialistic propositions, not always only to garner working-class votes. All of this is, or should be, well-known. "We are all Socialists now!" was the famous exclamation, in 1894, by Sir William Harcourt, an exemplary British Liberal, as Parliament was voting yet another bill of social reform. More than one hundred years later the entire globe is socialist, at least to the extent that the Welfare, or Provider, State has been accepted, at least in principle, and in varying modes of practice, throughout the world.

In this sense whether a government calls itself socialist or not is nearly irrelevant; but whether a government is nationalist or not is not irrelevant, not at all.

{POPULAR SOVEREIGNTY AND NATIONALISM}

S OON AFTER 1870 there appeared something else: a phenomenon whose evidences, here and there, were there earlier, but the breadth and the substance and the character of which began to change. This was modern and populist nationalism. Yet "nationalisme" and "nationaliste" became French words only after 1880; in Britain, too, they had appeared not much earlier. The reason for this relatively late gestation of the nationalist word was that "patriot" and "patriotism" already existed; and, at least for a while, it seemed that the meaning of the latter was sufficient. When, a century earlier, Samuel Johnson uttered his famous (and perhaps forever valid) dictum that Patriotism Is The Last Refuge Of A Scoundrel, he meant nationalism, even though that word did not yet exist. One of the reasons why there exists no first-rate book about the history of nationalism is that it is not easy to separate it from old-fashioned patriotism.* And these two inclinations, patriotism and nationalism, divergent as they may be, still often over-

---

* The other reason: nationalism may differ from country to country more than socialism or liberalism does. (That is, too, why histories of the Right are often more interesting than those of the Left.)

lap in people's minds. (When, for example, Americans criticize a "superpatriot," what they really mean is an extreme
nationalist.) Nonetheless, the very appearance of a new word
is always evidence that some people sense the need to distinguish it from the older word's meaning: that a nationalist is someone different from a patriot.

Patriotism is defensive; nationalism is aggressive. Patriotism is the love of a particular land, with its particular
traditions; nationalism is the love of something less tangible, of the myth of a "people," justifying many things, a
political and ideological substitute for religion. Patriotism
is old-fashioned (and, at times and in some places, aristocratic); nationalism is modern and populist. In one sense
patriotic and national consciousness may be similar; but in
another sense, more and more apparent after 1870, national
consciousness began to affect more and more people who,
generally, had been immune to that before—as, for example,
many people within the multinational empire of Austria-
Hungary. It went deeper than class consciousness. Here and
there it superseded religious affiliations, too.

After 1870 nationalism, almost always, turned antiliberal, especially where liberalism was no longer principally
nationalist. The contempt for the money-minded bourgeoisie that moved artists and writers a generation before
was now changing to a contempt for liberals. The great Nor-
wegian writer Knut Hamsun, for instance, hated not only
Gladstone, in whom he saw the prototype of a hypocrite and
a liberal, but all liberals. Confronted with someone whom

he suspected to be a liberal, "it is the logic in my blood expressing itself." Eventually this led Hamsun to become an unrepentant admirer of Hitler. Around 1890 William Traub, a Dutch radical, described the existing liberalism in Holland as "an old maid who will never flame into passionate fire, however long one may stroke her." To more and more people liberalism meant insufficient concern with the working classes; to others an insufficient nationalism and an excessive toleration of foreigners—and especially of those in their midst who pretended to belong to the national majority.

Because of this we ought to take a quick glance at the emergence of modern anti-Semitism. Here again 1870 is an important marker. The history of Jews and of their oppressions is of course a very long one; but now there came a change. The application of the term "anti-Semitism" to earlier people and events is imprecise and wrong. The very word appeared only around 1870. For nearly two thousand years before that we may speak of Judaeophobia but not of anti-Semitism. The origin and the justification of anti-Judaism was for a long time religious rather than racial. (Not always or wholly so: Judaeophobia in Spain, for instance, was religious in doctrine but more than often racial in practice.) However, anti-Semitism, all over Europe, latest after 1870, was no longer directed at the descendants of Christ-killers and Christ-deniers but at assimilating aliens in a nation's midst. It was fed by the appearance of successful Jews in many businesses and in certain professions, successful not only because of their guile in moneymaking but because of their ability to present themselves as true Germans or Austrians or Frenchmen, etc. (And often, the more assimilated, the worse.) "They are not like us . . ." Contempt and envy turning at times into outright hatred fueled anti-Semitism after 1870, with elements of suspicion and fear within it. Suspicion and fear: "Awake!" anti-Semites thought and preached. This, originally German, exclamation for a national awakening was employed by anti-Semites elsewhere too: wake from your slumber, rise up against the soulless ideas and institutions of liberalism, behind which crouch and lurk calculating Jews, pulling all kinds of strings, including International Capitalism and Free Trade. And behind International Socialism too.

{NATIONALISM AND SOCIALISM}

THE RELATIONSHIP of nationalism and socialism has been more complicated than that of nationalism and liberalism. By the twentieth century nationalists had little or nothing in common with liberals; but they had at least one thing in common with socialists: their opposition to and occasional hatred of international finan-

ciers and capitalists. Meanwhile, the numbers of voters and
the numbers of readers among the working classes were
growing. Their material conditions were not the primary
concerns of either conservatives or of liberals; but now
there existed socialists and Socialist parties. Yet what could
International Socialism offer to the masses? Wasn't their
sense of nationality, of their national belonging, at least as
strong and deep as their class consciousness? And how
about an international ideology and movement whose pro-
pagandists were often Jews? The time had come for a socialism that was national and "Christian." ("Christian" in this
sense meaning non-Jewish, among other vague categories.)
By 1890 various Christian Socialist parties and movements
appeared in Europe; and about ten years later came the first,
at that time still minuscule, Nationalist Socialist parties,
congregations, even National Socialist trade unions (especially within the German-speaking portions of the Austro-
Hungarian empire). They did not amount to much before
1914, but soon they would. Even before 1914 the radical socialist Mussolini realized that he was an *Italian* socialist: that
adjective not only modified the noun but it became dominant in his mind. After the war Hitler, who suddenly chose
to become a politician in 1919, recognized that nationalism
and socialism could and must be married, with the emphasis on the first. "I was a nationalist, and not a patriot," he
wrote about his youth in *Mein Kampf;* that he was a populist
socialist, not an international one, he would often say, later.
He was right: it was his nationalism rather than his social-

ism that congealed the majority of Germans, including those of the working classes, behind him, for twelve years, in victory and defeat, till the end. People, including his opponents, understood this. One, quite significant, proof of that is the history, or call it the emergence, of the word "Nazi." At first Hitler's National Socialists were called "the Nazi-Sozi," in a kind of abbreviated slang. Soon the "Sozi" was dropped, and the "Nazi" remained, a mark of its priority and predominance.

It is a great mistake to think that Hitler made (or was compelled to make) compromises with capitalism, that he was not a "real" socialist.* Not at all: he and his party condemned International Capitalism as much as they fought International Communism. And the history of the working classes throughout the twentieth century almost everywhere reveals that they will tolerate, and even admire successful capitalists—as long as they are capitalists of their kind of people.†

Mussolini, Hitler, Perón, Stalin: all of them nationalist socialists, with the emphasis on the first word. In 1870 and even decades later it seemed impossible that nationalism and socialism would ever be allied. Yet—considering the

---

*On one occasion he was supposed to have said, "Why should I nationalize the industries? I shall nationalize the people"—which is what he did.

†There are many examples of this, perhaps especially in the United States. But in National Socialist Germany too: among the Nazi leaders Hermann Göring, no matter how rich, opulent, and luxurious, was and remained most popular.

ubiquity of the welfare state—we are, at least in one sense, all national socialists now. Of course this conjunction of nationalism and socialism has varied from people to people; it could coexist with democratic institutions and with traditions of liberal freedom, as in many Scandinavian countries: German National Socialism was but one extreme variant that ended in disaster. But that the combination and the relationship (and the sometime quarrels and sometime marriages) of nationalism and socialism replaced the dialogues and debates between conservatives and liberals after 1870 is not to be doubted. The diverse combinations of nationalism and socialism marked most of the history of the twentieth century.

Of this the United States was, and remains, no exception. Rather the contrary. One reason why American parties named Socialist did not get very far was that the two great American political parties gradually espoused what in Europe were known as social welfare programs. But the main reason was that Socialists in America did not sound—or, indeed, did not seem—nationalist enough. During most of the nineteenth century, as we have seen, the conservative vs. liberal debate or dialogue in the United States did not really exist. But beginning in the twentieth century its nearly universal configuration did and does. Looking at this from a historical perspective, and using the proper terminology, we may say that generally speaking, in the United States the Republican Party has been more nationalistic than socialistic, while the Democrats have been more socialistic than nationalistic—the latter being perhaps the main cause of their relative decline during the last fifty years.

※

After the collapse of the Soviet Union the appeal and the reputation of Marx and of Marxism disappeared; but their decline well preceded the end of the Soviet empire, in many ways contrary to every Marxian dogma. The popular revolutions that began to shake the Soviet empire in Poland, Hungary, East Germany as early as in the 1950s were democratic and nationalist. More telling is the realization of the power of nationalism by the last Communist tyrants themselves, people such as Milosevic in Serbia or Ceauşescu in Romania. That was but a consequence of Marx's greatest failure, which was his profoundly mistaken concept of human nature (a concept not entirely different from that of capitalists, Progressives, liberals, economists, etc.): *homo oeconomicus,* Economic Man—when it became more and more evident that history was formed, and politics dependent upon, how and what large masses of people were thinking (and desiring, and fearing, and hating). That is: during the increasing intrusion of mind into matter.

We must not kick a man when he is down. Marx was an unattractive man but—at least intellectually—he was taking the side of the downtrodden and the poor, especially of the industrial workers (though not of peasants). Moreover, most of his critics miss the vital points, the inherent weaknesses of the Marxist body of dogma. The accepted intellectual or politological view is still that Marx was a utopian, that his ideas could hardly be put into practice, and when some leaders tried to do that, the result was an economic and humanitarian disaster. Much of that has been obvious. But we ought to look at Marx historically, not philosophically. Marx and Marxism failed well before 1989—not in 1956 and not in 1919 but in 1914. For it was then that internationalism and class consciousness melted away in the heat of nationalist emotions and beliefs. In 1914 there existed, for the first time, millions of members and voters of large internationally minded and class-conscious Socialist parties. Yet their opposition to a great war amounted to little or nothing; it had no real attraction, no force. The First World War marked the defeat of International Socialism; it led, instead, to the rise of National Socialism.

Marxists would never understand—let alone admit—this. They were (and many of them still are) thinking in categories of class consciousness instead of national consciousness. Marx was responsible for this, from the beginning. He entirely failed to understand what nationalism (beginning to rise all around him) was. His heavy, clumsy prose droned and thundered against Capitalism and against the State. Hardly a word about the Nation; and, of course, not even the slightest inkling (true, alas, of most political scientists even now) that State and Nation are not the same things. I shall have to return to this increasing dichotomy between nation and state later in this book (the man who understood this clearer than perhaps anyone else was Hitler). By 1914 national consciousness was so much stronger, so much more prevalent than was class consciousness. It is at least arguable that in 1914 a French worker had more in common with his capitalist or industrialist employer than with a German worker; the same thing was true of a German worker and of his employers.

But nationalism was (and remains) something more than a political ideology. Marx had not only ignored the element of "nation." There was another matter that he missed; indeed, that his philosophy of human nature was incapable of assessing. This was the desire of the working class for respectability. As the nineteenth century advanced, the material and often the social goals and aspirations and ambitions of the working classes became less and less different from those of the middle (and surely of the lower-middle) classes. Probably the wives of workingmen played an important part in this. The slow—all too slow, and in many ways inadequate—improvement of wages and of other material conditions made it possible for the wives of workers to give up their employment elsewhere and return to their modest homes as housewives. (Tocqueville foresaw something like this, too. He thought that with democracy advancing, more and more people would acquire their modicum of property that they would not endanger by responding to violent calls for revolution.) There was even more than that. Workingmen, and perhaps especially their wives, wished to be or to remain respected among their own. They were not inclined to seem insufficiently respectable or insufficiently national.

{THE ACCUMULATION OF OPINIONS}

THIS BRINGS US to what is perhaps the fundamental Marxist (and also economic; and often liberal) misreading of human nature. This is the—alas, still near-universally prevalent—belief that the world and its human beings consist of matter, and what the latter think and believe is but the superstructure of material "reality." But the opposite is true. Marx and other revolutionaries thundered against the monstrous practice and peril of the Accumulation of Capital (due to occur during the last critical phase of the Capitalist era). But what governs the world (and especially in the democratic age) is not the accumulation of money, or even of goods, but the accumulation of opinions. "Opinion governs the world": a profound truth, uttered by Pascal, more than three hundred and fifty years ago, in the age of the absolutist monarchy of Louis XIV. In the democratic age we are confronted with another enormous dimension of this reality: because the accumulation of opinions can be manufactured and even falsified through the machinery of publicity, at times even against contrary appearances. In the distant past political opinions were often private. Now they often are not.* That opinions can be molded, formed, falsified, inflated has always been true. But it is the accumulation of opinions that governs the history of states and of nations and of democracies as well as dictatorships in the age of popular sovereignty. It is the main ingredient of nationalisms, the cause of wars, and of the majority support of fanatical speakers like Hitler, or of the less enthusiastic but majoritarian support of less than mediocre presidents.

Opinions, convictions, ideas, beliefs are of course not the same, but they do overlap in the minds of many people, not less than in the past but perhaps especially at the end of the so-called Modern Age, when—contrary to the overall acceptance of the materialist concept of the world and of men—there is an increasing interference of mind with matter, indeed, its intrusion into matter. (That is why all philosophy must be epistemology now [another subject, though not an irrelevant one]). That is, too, why Freud, like Marx, must be recognized as antiquated. Again, we ought not kick at the memory of this otherwise serious thinker and stub our toes against the scrap-iron heap of his intellectual heritage. Again I must say a word about something that neither his critics nor his remaining followers have

---

*Which is why Machiavelli may be outdated; about this, too, see below, p. 181.

properly emphasized. Our concern—particularly for the purposes of this book—is not Freud's pan-sexualism. It is his emphasis, his invention of the subconscious. "Sub," not "un-"; beneath this we may detect something very Germanic, the belief that anything "deeper" is "truer." Yes, unconsciousness exists, it is always there in our minds, it is part of human life throughout. But our concern must be with the conscious mind: with what and how we, and other human beings, choose to think. And about that "how" (instead of "what" and "why") Freud tells us nothing.

It is not only that the "why" is so often latent in the "how." It is that in the age of popular sovereignty our concern must be with how people think, how they choose to think, including how they are influenced or impressed to think and speak. People who chose a police career in a state and society ruled by a Hitler or a Stalin were not necessarily "authoritarian personalities," a category invented by Freudian political sociologists. Such men chose a certain kind of career, and they adjusted their thinking and their behavior accordingly. So did those many thousands of Communists and intellectuals who chose not to believe, or even think about, the evidences of Soviet brutalities. Hatreds and fears are not subconscious phenomena. They exist within every human being. The difference between them is that there are people whose hatreds are more conscious than their fears, and others whose fears are more conscious than their hatreds. And both hatred and fear are inclinations and results not of the subconscious but of consciousness.

{PROGRESSIVE LIBERALISM}

FREUD, WHO DIED IN LONDON IN 1939, had lived to witness the power of Hitler and the rule of Stalin. From whatever evidence we have, Freud, like the vast majority of intellectuals, thought that what Hitler and his followers represented was something horribly atavistic and reactionary, reminiscent in some ways of the German Middle Ages. Most intellectuals, too, saw Communism representing an ideology of social utopia, though with doubtful results. At the bottom of their reasoning lay their belief in "Progress."

The history of the idea of Progress is not simple. Some appearances of its idea, or sentiment, undoubtedly existed in the remote past; but it must not be doubted that its still current idea emerged during the beginning of the Modern Age: not only because of its then-humanist optimism but because of a then-appearing historical consciousness. Eventually Progress meant Evolution; and Evolution, among other things, meant the evolving democratization of the world. It may be argued whether Freud was a committed progressive.* It is not arguable that Darwin so was. His *On the*

---

*He did believe in the progressive applicability of science to the study of mind and soul. He recognized criminality latent in human minds and hearts. Did he recognize sin?

Origin of Species was published in 1859, the year Tocqueville died. (Tocqueville despised the adjective *progressif,* which he called bad French. In one of his letters: "A religion is either true or not. How can it make progress?") Of course Marx cheered Darwin on. Of course Darwin was not an especially original thinker; his *Origins* fit very well into the intellectual climate of his times; it was (as accords with Victor Hugo's hoary maxim) An Idea Whose Time Had Come.* Of course most liberals were (and still are) Darwinists (almost from the beginning); conservatives less so (at least for a while). Of course this is not the place to question or criticize Darwinism—except to mention one profound and liberal contradiction. Liberalism, in its noblest and also in its most essential sense, had always meant (and, faintly, here and there it still means) an exaltation, a defense of the fundamental value and category of human dignity. Darwinism suggests that there was, there is, and there remains no fundamental difference between human beings and all other living beings. In sum: either human beings are unique or they are not. Either thesis may be credible but not both; and this is not merely a religious question.

However, my concern in this book is not with Darwinists but with Progressives. Darwin and Darwinism were part and parcel of the idea of Progress. And what did the idea of

---

*Allow me to state my conviction: An Idea Whose Time Has Come can seldom be any good. Allow me to add that this is not a result of intellectual snobbery, but a particular result of the state of communications in the mass democratic age.

Progress mean for society, rather than for science? It meant the extension of democracy further and further, across the globe. For a long time "Progress" was a Leftist slogan (the extreme nationalist slogan was, as we saw earlier: "Awake!"). In the beginning of the Modern Age the English use of the word "primitive" underwent a small but significant change: besides still meaning "ancient," "simple," "venerable" (as in "the primitive Church"), it began to be applied to people who were "behind" us (that is: behind us in time, not like, for the Greeks, "barbarians," who were "outside," incapable of being like us)—behind us not in space but in time, perhaps able to catch up with us, or at least with some of us, eventually. By the end of the Modern Age this once new concept of progress had become near-universal, to the extent that it was not absolutely dismissed, even by racists. Still, the main subject of this book is not the history of the idea of Progress but that of the democratization of much of the world; and the latter was predominantly an American idea.* The ideals, appeals, impulses of Progress and democratization were of course connected—indeed, at times, to the extent of their inseparability. By the end of the nineteenth century the Progressive movement—indeed, the existence of Progressivism in politics—was specifically American. It is therefore that it requires a cursory examination.

*As a perhaps unduly broad and surely imprecise generalization it may be said that while the (especially nineteenth-century) British ideal was the liberalization of much of the world, the American ideal was its democratization.

The American belief in, the sometimes American obsession with "Progress" is very old; it was there from the beginning, when it was more than merely latent but expressed by Puritan preachers and spokesmen (in inherent contradiction with their idea of sinfulness that then evaporated fast).* But it was not until about 1880 that a consequence of this appeared on the surface of politics, with some people—concerned and serious Republicans, mostly from New England—calling themselves Progressives. They reacted against what to them seemed the stagnant and corrupt materialism of the Republican Party. They were a minority; but soon their ideas and their influence grew wider and wider. American liberal Protestantism was wholly allied with them. By the end of the nineteenth century the Progressivism of most of the American liberal churches preceded the actual (though temporary) appearance of a Progressive Party in 1912. It is amazing how unquestioningly and enthusiastically American Protestants embraced Darwinism.† This ought to tell us

---

*Another inherent contradiction—now with democracy—was Emerson's belief that "the progress of culture" depended on small "minorities," "a few superior and attractive men," forming a "knighthood" of learning and virtue ("The Progress of Culture," 1867).

†Here the—still largely accepted—interpretation by Richard Hofstadter is wrong. In his *The Age of Reform* he called the American capitalists and materialists of the Republican Party "Social Darwinists." They were not that—or, more precisely, only partly so. Social Darwinism is an inadequate designation. Just about every American, including moneybags, believed in "progress"—that is, in natural and incontrovertible evolution. Yet the Survival of the Fittest was a typically German rather than an American article of belief.

something about the shallowness of their religious beliefs, together with their belief in the progress of democracy. Here are but a few, random but telling, examples. The title of the books written by one of their then-foremost public figures, the Rev. Lyman Abbott: *The Evolution of Christianity* in 1892; *The Theology of an Evolutionist* in 1897. Another prominent Protestant churchman, William Jewett Tucker, wrote around the same time: "The term which best expresses the character of the modernizing process . . . is the term 'progressive.'" In 1903 the *Encyclopedia Americana* stated that "progress governed the whole natural and moral universe." The Rev. Shailer Matthews, dean of the University Chicago's Divinity School, a celebrated public theologian (and an imbecile): "St. Augustine's philosophy held no attraction to the modern world; outdated, it could not account for factors so visibly directing the course of events." Or: "The modern man of any period. . . is controlled by the forces which are making progress." "The church, therefore, had to prepare the way." "In every area of life the progressive clergy preached the wonders of 'tomorrow.'"* Another theologian, Walter Rauschenbuch: "Progress [is] divine." American liberal Protestantism, together with American intellectuality, was enthusiastic about America's choices

*See the excellent book by Richard Gamble, *The War for Righteousness: Progressive Christianity, the Great War, and the Rise of the Messianic Nation* (Wilmington, 2003), 50, from which I took some of the citations in this paragraph.

for war. The abovementioned Lyman Abbott in 1898, of the American war against Spain: "a crusade for brotherhood." Thus liberal Protestants promoted and cheered on America's entry into the First World War. *The Independent,* a magazine founded by Plymouth Church (note this church's name, harking back to its Puritan origins): The days of kings "are numbered. The monarchs will go—and they will." On the day of Wilson's declaration of war against Germany, which happened on Good Friday, Edward Stires, pastor of a fashionable Fifth Avenue church: "Something more than coincidence. Today our Easter faith goes into action." The president of Brown University, 1918: "The Central Powers believe that government by the people 'is government by the gutter,' and we . . . believe that 'the voice of the people is the voice of God.'" A Herbert R. Willett, editor of *The Christian Century,* at the end of the war: "The Kingdom of Heaven is at hand." "The conception of God as a monarch, all-powerful, remote, transcendent and autocratic is no longer suited to the needs or the comprehension of the modern mind." Professor George Coe, associate of John Dewey, professor in the Union Seminary: "The phrase 'democracy of God' replaced the 'kingdom of Hope.' Jesus's teaching offered mankind the divine-human democracy as a final social ideal." The Methodist minister Worth M. Tippy in 1919: "The forces of democracy will invade and rebuild every institution of the world." In 1922 Harry Emerson Fosdick, a celebrated and leading Protestant during many decades: Christianity must now decide "what its attitude shall be toward this new and powerful force, the idea of Progress, which in every realm is remaking man's thinking." Christianity is needed to come "to intelligent terms with this dominant idea." Dominant? New? Powerful? 1922: Mussolini coming to power; Hitler rising; Wilson (and Lenin) half-dead. By 1922 a reaction against such shibboleths—in Europe, England, and even among some American writers—had already begun.*

Did these liberal Protestants believe what they were saying? Probably, yes. But we cannot blame them only. There are masses of evidence proving that Woodrow Wilson believed just about everything they were saying; that Theodore Roosevelt at least some part of it; that most American Catholics believed it too. So did Henry Ford as much as John Dewey, and the biblical literalist William Jennings Bryan as well as his self-proclaimed agnostic opponent Clarence Darrow. But my subject is not American intellectual or religious history. In any event—eighty years later the bleating sounds of these cracked trumpets sound even more ridiculous—and, yes, even more contemptible—than be-

---

*Chesterton, *circa* 1922: "Progress began in boredom; and, heaven knows, it sometimes seems likely to end in it. And no wonder: of all other falsehoods the most false, I think, is this notion that men can be happy in movement, when nothing but dullness drives them on from behind. . . . It is the great progressive proposition; that he must seek for enjoyment because he has lost the power to enjoy. . . . A hunger for civilisation . . . is an appetite not easily appreciated now, when people are so overcivilised that they can only have a hunger for barbarism."

fore:* when, even among Americans, the unquestioning belief in Progress is becoming fainter; and when remaining liberals as well as those few who are not superficial conservatives no longer maintain an unquestioning trust in the benefits of technological progress. And we ought to recognize that trust and belief in technology were unbroken, indeed, enthusiastically embraced by men such as Hitler and Goebbels[†]—who were populists.

---

*Consider Ronald Reagan, 1982: America's "divine destiny" is to reaffirm this nation's special calling; George W. Bush in 2002 about "Progress": America is "the hope of all mankind." 12 December 2001: "America must fight the enemies of Progress." Etc., etc.

[†]Goebbels in 1939: "We live in an age that is both romantic and steely. The bourgeois were alien and hostile to technology, skeptics believed that the roots of the collapse of European culture lay in it. National Socialism has understood how to take the soulless framework of technology and fill it with the rhythm and hot impulses of our time."

A S OF NATIONALISM, no history of populism exists—except, here and there, of its American political variant. The idea of populism is of course very old. Populist revolts, populist leaders are scattered throughout the history of Europe, before, during, and after the Protestant Reformation; and perhaps especially in England. They were, almost always, antiaristocratic; but they were not always of the "Left." There was a strong populist element, racist rather than nationalist, among the Spanish people who turned against Jews and compelled the royal government to expel most of the latter (and to examine the spiritual "essence" of converted Jews through the instrument of the Spanish Inquisition); there was a populist element among those Dutchmen who rebelled against the Spaniards and Catholics in the Netherlands; the Levellers and most radical Puritans were populists before, during, and after the English Civil War. During the birth of the United States, Shays's Rebellion and the Whiskey Rebellion were populist (though perhaps tribal and local). The French counterrevolutionaries in the Vendée, too, were largely populist. So were the different right-wing popular movements against the French and their followers in Spain and Italy, during Napoleon's era.

But these "reactionary" outbursts of popular sentiments were not—yet—nationalist.* Then, again around 1870, there came a change. Populism, like Progressivism, struggled for an ever wider and deeper extension of democracy. (Some respect is due to the honesty of certain American Populists, especially in states such as Minnesota.) Both Progressives and Populists believed that true democracy had become thwarted by the constricting powers of moneyed interests, corrupt capitalists and politicians, and so on. But there was, from the beginning, a fatal difference between Progressives and Populists. They were different kinds of people. In the United States the Progressives, starting to form about 1880, were men and women concerned with what they saw as the self-satisfied materialism of the ruling Republican Party, consisting of politicians whom the Progressives saw as hopelessly vulgar and backward. These intellectual and social and political reformers (called "mugwumps" by their "conservative" Republican opponents, who called themselves "stalwarts") were often upper-class Amer-

---

*Owen Chadwick: "These guerilla wars of peasants often had religion as their flag. How far they really fought for their Church, or for their local church, or for a sacred object within their church, is now impossible to determine. As in the 'wars of religion' during the age of Reformation, the defence of a way of worship was one, and seldom the most important, motive for taking up arms. They would never take up weapons because French or republicans closed a neighbouring monastery, or abolished a college of canons, or impoverished their bishop. They were more disturbed at the destruction of their brotherhoods, much more disturbed if a popular feast were silenced or a miracle-working picture removed."

icans, almost always Protestants, most of them New Eng-
landers. They believed in social and political planning—that
is, a reform of society propagated by them, coming from
above. The Populists mostly came from the Midwest and
the South, they believed in reform (and, on occasion, in revolution) arising from the lower classes. (Not from the very
lowest: because, especially in the South, the Populists stood
with extreme rigidity against the social and political rights
of blacks; here and there, they opposed immigrants, too.)
Another decade later came another gradual change. The
Democratic Party—mostly, though not exclusively, because
of its strength in the South—included and absorbed the Populists, whose political party, by and large, disappeared (again,
except in Minnesota). At the same time the Democratic
Party began to appeal to the industrial working class as well
as to most immigrants. By about 1910 (though not yet in the
South), they had become, by and large, the more liberal
party of the two. Meanwhile Progressivism had—or at least
seems to have had—triumphed: Theodore Roosevelt was a
Progressive, Woodrow Wilson was a Progressive, Herbert
Hoover was a Progressive. And there was another element.
By 1900, latest by 1910, there was a change in the composition of the Progressives. They were no longer mostly reform-
minded and thoughtful Republicans of the upper classes.
American intellectuals and what may be called the American intelligentsia—a new phenomenon, a class marked not
by their social provenance but by their ideas and opinions—

were, with very few exceptions, proponents and partisans of political and social reforms—in one word, progressives.

However: these liberal intellectuals and professionals and liberal Protestant churchmen still believed in political and social reforms from above. They regarded themselves, surely mentally, as superior to "the people" whom they wished (or at least thought they wished) to assist and reform. (This kind of intellectual myopia, or split-mindedness—often to the extent of dishonesty—was also typical of those intellectuals, extreme progressives, who in 1930 and thereafter joined the Communist Party or were at least sympathetic fellow-travellers of it.) They saw themselves as the evident members of a new ruling class, of an intellectual and political rather than a social or economic elite; thus they would be the leaders of great political movements whom people would, or would have to, follow. Their other flaw—more enduring in its consequences—was the progressives' propositions and achievements of electoral and other political reforms. During the 1910s opposition to their political and social ideas was not strong enough, so that they could push through (and within the American constitutional process this was no easy thing)—constitutional amendments: for instance the primary election of senators, the aim of which was to further democratize the political process, to make it more rational, less restricted. They were convinced that a further and further extension of democracy meant, inevitably and naturally, further guarantees and extensions of liberty. The very opposite happened: primaries—and, later, their further application to the selection of presidential candidates—compromised and vulgarized the political process, making it even worse than before, on many occasions aiding demagogues, and on virtually every occasion transforming already dubious contests of popularity into publicity contests.

We have seen how the entry of the United States into World War I was marked by what seemed an overwhelming triumph of the Progressives. But that was deceiving. Already during the war there were signs of a division between Populists and Progressives. Many Populists—especially in states of the Midwest with large German and Scandinavian populations—opposed the war. Another constitutional amendment in the late 1910s, the Prohibition one, marked a triumph of mostly antiliberal Protestantism (even though there were Progressives who supported it too). Then, during the Twenties, the former alliance between Progressives and Populists faded away. Some of the top figures of the American twenties were Populists as well as Progressives—for example, Henry Ford or Calvin Coolidge—but the Dayton monkey trial in 1925 pitted William Jennings Bryan, the Great Populist, defending the Bible against evolution, against Clarence Darrow, the Chicago Progressive, defending science against the Bible. In some midwestern and western states populist legislatures passed laws that horrified (justly) liberals, proposing censorships of textbooks, and preaching a narrow and extreme nationalism. By 1930 an image of populists was represented by Grant Wood's *American Gothic:* a painting of a thin-lipped, embittered farming couple, the man holding a pitchfork in his hand. A few years later the divorce of Populists and Progressives was final. Huey Long, Charles Coughlin, most isolationists, etc., were Populists. They represented the greatest political danger to Franklin Roosevelt. The remaining old Progressives were internationalists, while the Populists were nationalists—indeed, American national socialists of a kind.*

---

*Again Richard Hofstadter in *Anti-Intellectualism in American Life* was wrong. He identified Populism with anti-intellectualism. Not quite: then, as now, American (as also other) populists would venerate certain intellectuals whom they saw as their own. (The quintessential populist Joseph McCarthy called some of his targets "pseudointellectuals"—that is, not "real" intellectuals.) Even more telling: despite their dislike of capitalists, populists in every country respected and supported millionaires of their own kind. (Nationalist, not internationalist, capitalists of course.)

{POPULIST ANTI-SEMITISM AND GERMANOPHILIA}

B
UT THIS HAPPENED IN AMERICA fifty years after Europe. There, throughout most of the nineteenth century, and in many places also thereafter, the evocation of The People was a leftist, socialist, and occasionally communist practice. *Le Peuple, Populaire, Volksstimme,* etc., were Socialist newspapers and publications.* But by 1914 the nationalist Mussolini named his new newspaper *Popolo d'Italia,* and ten years later Hitler his *Völkischer Beobachter.* (In the 1930s a French Fascist publication, *L'Ami du peuple,* named itself after Marat's 1789 rag.)

In most instances this new appeal, this new evocation of "the people," included three elements. One was xenophobia, with its particular kind of anti-Semitism; the second was nationalism; yet another the influence of Germany. A prototype of this populism was the Austrian one. Throughout the nineteenth century the numbers of Jews in Austria (and especially in Vienna) were increasing; more

*Some—but only some—of this survived in the twentieth century (example: the official names of Communist-ruled states in the Soviet sphere after 1945: "People's Democracies").

significant, there was evidence of their growing presence in certain professions, and especially in the press. In Austria, too, dislike was no longer principally directed against the presence of Orthodox and religious Jews but against assimilated and often no longer strictly religious ones. For most educated Jews (and to most liberal non-Jews) assimilation was desirable. It meant their identification with a state where they had been born, or where they had come to live and stay; it was to be the logical and natural consequence of their legal and political equality. But for anti-Semites, especially after 1870, the assimilated Jews were more of an enemy and a greater danger than were the Orthodox Jews who were recognizable by their weird and often unpleasant appearance and habits, obviously alien people visible to the naked eye. The influences—indeed, the very identities—of the assimilated Jew were not always and not easily visible; and the people—one's own people, all classes of the nation— must be awakened to that. Such was (and remains) the essence of modern anti-Semitism: yes, it was racial but, even more, it was spiritual.* It was a reaction of anti-Semites, instinctive and not entirely unnatural or artificial, against what they saw as a not-always-visible but, consequently, insidious influence of Jews and of their allies in the spiritual

---

*Hitler, too—contrary to almost all accepted opinion, including that of scholars and of his biographers—was less a racist than an extreme nationalist. On one occasion he said that Jews were not a physical but a spiritual race. (See my *The Hitler of History* [New York, 1997].)

and mental life of the nation: an alien and at least potentially toxic element, a dangerous solvent weakening, if not
altogether destroying, the spiritual essence of their nation.

Liberalism, to most people, meant philo-Semitism. But
it also seemed to more and more people, including some
well-meaning ones, that liberalism, the cult of liberty and of
equality, was destroying the order of the world. Thus many
of the anti-Semites after 1870 were conservatives: but their
conservatism was a new kind, with its populist sense. Consider the language—and the tone!—of a Catholic and conservative publication, the *Vaterland*, when a principal Vienna liberal newspaper, the *Neues Wiener Tagblatt*, lost a
court case in 1885: "The people have spoken: and the voice
of the people is the voice of God!" (No conservative would
have said anything like this before.) "The terrorists of the
Jewish press are condemned, and their rule of horror is
coming to an end!"*

Thus, about one hundred and twenty years ago, in Austria the classic nineteenth-century contest between conservatives and liberals began to be superseded by a third force,
which in Austria called itself Christian (meaning antiliberal
and anti-Jewish) Socialist (which meant nationalist and not

---

*Cited in Brigitte Hamann, *Rudolf* (Vienna, 1991). There are many
such examples of this, among them the name of a new Austrian Catholic newspaper: *Österreichischer Volksfreund*—The Austrian people's friend.
Or consider the archconservative Archduke Albrecht, warning his relative, the outspokenly liberal Crown Prince Rudolf: "*Liberal* once meant
a generous and magnanimous great noble; and now?"

international socialist). In Vienna the Christian Socialists swept into power in the 1890s on a wave of populist anti-liberalism and anti-Semitism (the latter became thereafter mitigated by their charismatic leader, the Vienna mayor Karl Lueger). What was significant in this then virulent anti-liberal and anti-Jewish rhetoric was that its propagators and adherents were no longer conservative or aristocratic or traditionalist. They were not reactionary but populist. "Volk" and "völkisch," "people" and "populist" were no longer words of the Left. Eventually this populist rhetoric contributed to the fatal crises of the Habsburg empire; and its influence soon spread to people next to Austria. It had a powerful impact on the mind of the young Hitler, who—we must not forget—was not German-born but Austrian, and who incarnated many Austrian manners, inclinations, and habits throughout his life.

※

What happened in Austria during the last two decades of the nineteenth century was more significant than the contemporary Dreyfus affair in France. The Dreyfus case—in spite of its still prevalent and repetitious reputation—was not really a populist phenomenon. (For one thing, it left masses of French workers largely indifferent.)

For the last time I must write something about the history of modern anti-Semitism. I must clarify the categories—more precisely: its tendencies. Populism was (and remains) inevitably nationalist. It was (and is) often anti-Semitic, though not inevitably so. Conservatives were and are often more anti-Semitic than are liberals; but, again, not inevitably so. (The best among them, during the twentieth century, have been principled opponents of anti-Semitism, horrified by the persecution and suppression and murder of Jews.) One hundred years ago a reactionary and conservative and religious kind of Judaeophobia still existed. This is largely extinct now in the West; but it was there in France both before and during and even after the Dreyfus case: Judaeophobia, rather than anti-Semitism, for many reasons, social and religious, rather than populist or national ones. Its main element was fear of the presence and influence of Jews; and when it erupted into hatred, that was the consequence of a deeper latent fear. (The opposite would be the case of Hitler.)

In 1886 there appeared a book in Paris by Edouard Drumont, a Catholic and a conservative, entitled *La France juive,* Jewish France. (It is difficult to find now; it has disappeared from many of the largest libraries of the world.) His argument was that the political and intellectual life of the Third Republic has been infiltrated and populated and now largely governed by Jews. Drumont followed this with another, even less known and less available book, in 1888: *La fin d'un monde,* The end of a world. His theme was now more than a startling recognition of the pervasive influence of Jews in the intellectual and political and social life of Paris (in that descending order of importance): but that such a perni-

cious influence meant nothing less than the end of a world, of an entire world, of Christian France, of a world that was once governed by Christians. (For a time the book sold well, not only in France but in Austria and in Germany.) Now Drumont's fury was directed less against Jews than against Frenchmen and Frenchwomen and other European Christians who did not see and who did not oppose this.*
Drumont, attacked and vilified, was soon disregarded and his book forgotten. Still, that took some time, and in 1895 came an explosive example of French Judaeophobia in the case against Dreyfus. And before the case against Dreyfus collapsed—that took more than a few years—Judaeophobia intoxicated many people in France: many Catholics, many of the remnant aristocrats, officers, conservatives, students.

Yet the anti-Dreyfusards were not populists. The rising and influential right-wing party and movement, Charles Maurras's Action Française, appeared around that time. Maurras was a monarchist, antirepublican as well as anti-democratic. ("Democracy is government by mere numbers," he wrote.) His clear and cutting prose style was ad-

---

*Austria-Hungary, Drumont wrote, "is even more judaized than France." Numerically this was so. He attacked the liberal Crown Prince Rudolf and his coterie. A few months after the publication of Drumont's book, on 30 January 1889, Rudolf killed himself and his ephemeral paramour Maria Vetsera in the castle of Mayerling. A few months later, in a small town on the border of Austria and Germany, Adolf Hitler was born. Forty-four years after the day of Mayerling, on 30 January 1933, Hitler was made chancellor of the German Reich, with the help of German conservatives.

mired by many French intellectuals. His hatred of Jews caused France (and ultimately him) a great deal of harm. But we must recognize that the anti-Dreyfusards and the Action Française were, truly, "extreme right-wing," not populist, not a totalitarian phenomenon, not at all national socialist, and not of course pro-German—even as their influence would one day work in favor of Germany and of Hitler, alas.

A generation later, in 1931, Georges Bernanos wrote a book, admiring and regretting the fate of Drumont: *La grande peur des bien-pensants,* The great fear of the well-meaning—that is, of the conformists, very much including Catholics and nominal Catholics, people who had attempted nervously to ignore Drumont. Bernanos's fury was aimed not at the Jews but at the cowardice of Frenchmen. Bernanos was a profound Catholic, a traditionalist, a patriot—but a nationalist not at all. Indeed, "nationalism" he called "that collective greed of nationalism, which perverts the notion of Fatherland into the idol of A People's State." Few have seen the evil genius, the danger of Hitler, clearer than Bernanos. (A man who saw this quality of Bernanos was Charles de Gaulle.)

Patriots and nationalists; reactionaries and populists— evidences that these are not mental cerebrations or semantic distinctions exist throughout the Second World War. They are there in France, in the record of French National Socialists during (and also before and after) that war. They put their faith, their hopes and their wishes, in Germany's victory. They hoped for a nationalist revolution, not an authoritarian restoration. The latter was more the case of Vichy France, about whom the French National Socialists often wrote with venom, brilliantly at times: Vichy was outdated, full of old women, surrounded by their dusty bibelots, greedy clerics, and the odor of cat piss. (And there was some truth in this—the weakness of conservatives, whether the French Pétain or the German Papen or, say, the Ohioan Taft: their fear of the Left and their consequent unwillingness and inability to separate themselves from the extreme nationalists—yes, as with all human categories and definitions, the distinctions between patriots and nationalists are seldom absolute.) But here I wish to draw attention to a tendency, to an element which was at work within and among the French and European national socialists which has not received adequate attention. This was the influence and the attraction of Germany, something that cannot and must not be simply attributed to collaborationist opportunism during the war. The most brilliant collaborationist intellectual Robert Brasillach spat out this challenge at his trial for treason in 1945: "We have slept with the Germans, and liked much of it." It may be that this was why Charles de Gaulle refused to commute Brasillach's death sentence, despite the petitions of some leading French intellectuals. (More than fifty years later, in our very times, Jean-Marie Le Pen's Front National venerates Brasillach.) And sixty years after 1945 a common denominator of just about *all* extreme nationalist parties and movements across the world, in such different countries as Italy or Hungary or Romania or Belgium or

Argentina or even the United States is their often apparent admiration for Hitler's Germany, the once (or forever?) true Third Force of the world, transcending capitalism and communism.

While during the nineteenth century republicanism, across Europe, included Francophilia, after the First World War nationalism, in many places, often meant being pro-German. (Already in the 1890s the New England Progressives were, largely, Anglophiles; the Populists often Anglophobes.) During World War II there was a division, running across the most diverse societies and places in the world, between Anglophiles and Germanophiles: the upper middle classes were often Anglophile, the lower middle classes pro-German. National Socialist Germany was young; the liberal democracies, not to speak of their monarchies and aristocracies, were old . . .

And now one more word about the phenomenon of modern nationalism, inseparable as that is from the recognition of the difference between nation and state.

THE STATE WAS ONE of the creations of the Modern Age. Its powers grew; here and there, sooner or later, it became monstrously bureaucratic. Yet—and few people see this, very much including those who prattle about "totalitarianism"—the power of the state has been weakening, at the same time the attraction of nationalism has not.

Hitler knew that: I have, more than once, cited his sentence from *Mein Kampf* recalling his youth: "I was a nationalist; but I was not a patriot." Again it is telling that in Austria "national" and "nationalist" meant pro-German, and not only during the multinational Habsburg monarchy and state. Well before the Second World War an Austrian "nationalist" wanted some kind of union with Germany, at the expense of an independent Austrian state. This was also true in such diverse places as Norway or Hungary or other states during the Second World War: "national" and "nationalist" often meant pro-German.

Nationalism, rather than patriotism; the nation rather than the state; populism rather than liberal democracy, to be sure. We have examples of that even among the extremist groups in the United States, too, with their hatred of "government"—that is, of the state. We have seen that while true patriotism is defensive, nationalism is aggressive; patri-

otism is the love of a particular land, with its particular traditions; nationalism is the love of something less tangible,
of the myth of a "people," justifying everything, a political
and ideological substitute for religion; both modern and
populist. An aristocratic nationalism is an oxymoron, since
at least after the late seventeenth century most European
aristocracies were cosmopolitan as well as national. Democratic nationalism is a later phenomenon. For a while there
was nothing very wrong with that. It won great revolutions
and battles, it produced some fine examples of national co-
hesion. One hundred and fifty years ago a distinction between nationalism and patriotism would have been labored,
it would have not made much sense. Even now nationalism
and patriotism often overlap within the minds and hearts of
many people. Yet we must be aware of their differences—
because of the phenomenon of populism which, unlike
old-fashioned patriotism, is inseparable from the myth of a
people. Populism is folkish, patriotism is not. One can be
a patriot and cosmopolitan (certainly culturally so). But a
populist is inevitably a nationalist of sorts. Patriotism is less
racist than is populism. A patriot will not exclude a person
of another nationality from a community where they have
lived side by side and whom he has known for many years;
but a populist will always be suspicious of someone who
does not seem to belong to his tribe.

A patriot is not necessarily a conservative; he may even be
a liberal—of sorts, though not an abstract one. In the twentieth century a nationalist could hardly be a liberal. The nine-

teenth century was full of liberal nationalists, some of them inspiring and noble figures. The accepted view is that liberalism faded and declined because of the appearance of socialism, that the liberals who originally had reservations about exaggerated democracy became democrats and then socialists, accepting the progressive ideas of state intervention in the economy, education, welfare. This is true but not true enough. It is nationalism, not socialism, that killed the liberal appeal. The ground slipped out from under the liberals not because they were not sufficiently socialist but because they were (or at least seemed to be) insufficiently nationalist.

Since it appeals to tribal and racial bonds, nationalism seems to be deeply and atavistically natural and human. Yet the trouble with it is not only that nationalism can be anti-humanist and often inhuman but that it also proceeds from one abstract assumption about human nature itself. The love for one's people is natural, but it is also categorical; it is less charitable and less deeply human than the love for one's country, a love that flows from traditions, at least akin to a love of one's family. Nationalism is both self-centered and selfish—because human love is not the love of oneself; it is the love of *another*.* Patriotism is always more than merely biological—because charitable love is human and not merely "natural." Nature has, and shows, no charity.

---

*A convinced nationalist is suspicious not only of people he sees as aliens; he may be even more suspicious of people of his own ilk and ready to denounce them as "traitors"—that is, people who disagree with his nationalist beliefs.

2

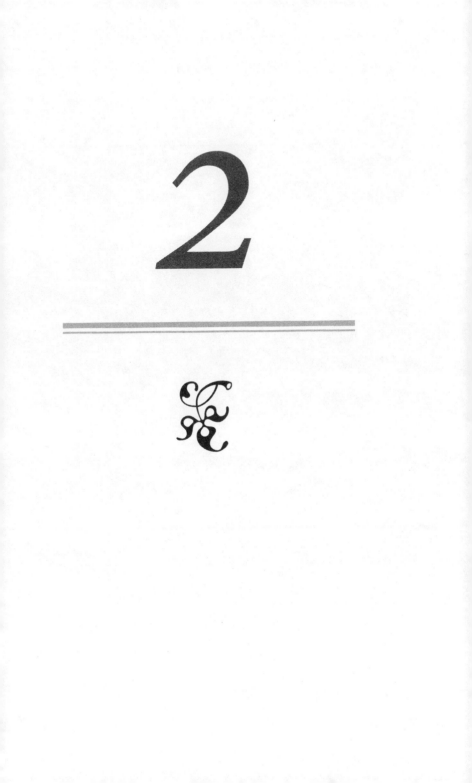

{1914: THE WORLD OF YESTERDAY?}

REMNANTS OF old-fashioned patriotism (so often inseparable from gentlemanly behavior) existed and even survived the catastrophe of the First World War. But the great tides of nationalism and of populism preceded the war, dominated it, reached unprecedented peaks after it and then during the Second World War. After that their strength seemed to abate—somewhat, here and there—but kept on existing, often underneath and not on the visible surface of events. We are not near the end of it, not at all.

But let us look, once more, at 1914, and at the world before it. Let us begin with a contradictory impression. In the numberless memoirs and in the memories of so many sensitive men the Great War came suddenly, an unexpected boom of thunder, a flash of lightning from a blue sky. Yet serious historians and also other people, those who filled entire shelves of libraries with their studies about the origins of the war, knew that the skies over Europe had been heavy with ominous clouds in 1914 and well before it; that, in a way, what was surprising was not that war came but that it had not come earlier. And that is more than an impression: it belongs to the diplomatic history of the period, to the history of the relations of states.

There is one explanation of this contradiction. Those statesmen, diplomatists, politicians, generals, rulers who decided for war if war must come envisaged a war very different from what then came. Their miscalculations are evident; they existed, in one way or another, in every counsel of every state in 1914.

But every human event has multiple causes; and the cause-effect relationship in human events does not accord with the cause-effect relations in mechanical causality. And it is not really enough to ascertain the pathogenesis of events (as, too, in the case of physical illnesses); we must also attempt to find something about their etiology. But there we often cannot go much further or deeper than to recognize some of the symptoms of causes. Here we must question the—natural and valuable and not really shortsighted and widely accepted and even enduring—views of those who looked and still look back at the world before 1914 as a Golden Age; and, consequently, at the First World War as one of the greatest catastrophes in the history of mankind (well, at least of European mankind). There is truth in that vision of that Golden Age—as, for example, in Stefan Zweig's *The World of Yesterday,* a fine book—but not quite enough.

We ought to admit that much of The World of Yesterday (at the time of this writing that is a world of two or three generations before our yesterdays) was ugly. Fashions, clothes, decorations, interiors; the wretched industrial circumstances of the working masses, the dark backstreets of the great cities as well as the high society enclosures, the atmosphere of their circumstances—yes, there was a breakaway from the heaviness of late Victorianism and from the heavy drapery of the bourgeoisie, but not much. Society was insecure. Edwardianism was an improvement over Victorianism, but a thin one. Society was not only insecure but unsure of itself—not because of its rigidity but because of its increasing fluidity. The Edwardian years were racier, sunnier than the Victorian years had been, but they could not last. A few historians saw this (consider but the title of George Dangerfield's excellent book, *The Strange Death of Liberal England*); but all of that went deeper and spread wider than the existence and the symptoms of anarchism, socialism, strikes, social unrest, gnawing away at the capitalist order (or disorder) before 1914. Social mobility was accelerating—including the rise of many Jews to higher and higher levels, or at least to higher institutions of society. Social anti-Semitism was but a superficial and hypocritical response to that. But even social anti-Semites regarded the existence of national and popular anti-Semitism as but a backward remnant of ancient prejudices, unpleasant responses from a past. They were wrong. In sum: nothing lasts forever; but the World Before 1914 could not have lasted long, world war or not.

Historians' debates about the origins of the First World War still go on and on. Their concern is to affix, properly, the responsibility—or, more accurately, the distribution of responsibilities—for the outbreak of the war, according to governments. Emperors, tsars, kings; prime ministers, foreign ministers, war ministers; admirals, generals, chiefs of staff; ambassadors, envoys, etc., etc. The then-still-semiaristocratic and upper-class system of Europe's states miscalculated: a stunning case of Unintended Consequences. That we know; we also know that generations blamed them after the war, understandably so. They had chosen war—some of them quite willingly, some of them more reluctantly, though it soon turned out to be not the war they had wanted, or thought of. But there is something about 1914 that has not received sufficient attention, except here and there. Yes, 1914 *seemed* the last time when millions of men were driven to slaughter and into catastrophes by their self-centered rulers, or even by the powers of fading and rotting upper classes. But: did not these millions of men go to war willingly, enthusiastically? They were as wrong about the war as were their rulers. Both they and their rulers thought in terms of the last wars they remembered or knew about, short wars of 1870 or of the 1900s or even after. But that was not all. The peoples of 1914 were not the peoples of 1870. They were more, not less, nationalist than the generations before them. Because of the progress of compulsory education and literacy they, even most of the lower classes, read newspapers. The responsibilities of the various national newspapers in and before 1914 remain to be examined. There ought to be ample room for thoughtful and profound readings and comparisons of the French and German and Austrian and British and Russian, etc., newspapers and of their rhetoric (not to speak of the American press in and before 1917). "Rhetoric": because it is not merely that thought results in words; speech, slogans, words reverberate into thought; indeed, often they create thought. The newspapers (and many other publications) in 1914, their owners and editors and journalists, were as responsible for the coming catastrophe as were short-sighted ambassadors or martinets or ministers. And so were their readers, the masses of Europe's peoples, who not only largely believed what they read in the papers but whose nationalism was the faith that had penetrated their minds, indeed, their hearts—a substitute religion whose roots were not new but whose fervency was: an intrusion of minds into the structure of events, an element of which the rulers of their states were aware.

The study of rhetoric in 1914 may be overdue; at any rate it is describable and even definable. Less definable is the—transitory—state and extent of the enthusiasm with which so many men answered the call to arms in 1914. That, too, was a symptom of the cracking of the old order well before 1914. The bourgeois ways of life well before 1914 were uninspiring and boring. Going into a national war was, for many young men, a relief. Within that sense of relief there also lay a—proper and approved and evident—sentiment of hatred. To hate one's nation's enemies was better, healthier, safer than to hate the corruptions of one's social order (or disorder). Nationalist hatred was better than class hatred. Among the rulers and governments of states who decided war in 1914, the dominant feeling was less hatred than it was fear: the fear that if they do not, however reluctantly, choose war *now*, then their governments and states run unforeseeable and terrifying risks. These fears and hatreds then led to horrific consequences. But—perhaps—we may risk the thought that while those who fear may be as much responsible for their consequences as those who hate, the counselors and purveyors of fear are (and were) not necessarily worse than the propagators and purveyors of hatred.

The First World War (as almost every war) was of course full of unintended consequences. One of these was the big surge toward the further democratization of the world.

There were people (some of their names are well-known) who before 1914 pronounced that wars, especially great wars, were becoming impossible, or at least implausible. Implausible, because of their cost, wrote a Russian Jewish financier (Ivan S. Bloch); his argument seemed to have impressed the tsar himself, but also others; and it had some influence on some international organizations (for example, on the International Court of Justice at The Hague) during the first decade of the twentieth century. Implausible: because of political and social progress that brought the participation of entire populations in the governing decisions of their states; thus wrote Norman Angell, an English liberal philosopher in 1912. They were wrong. The young Winston Churchill wrote well before 1914 that the wars of peoples will be more terrible than the wars of monarchies in the past. This of course happened in 1914, and increasingly in the terrible years that followed, when entire peoples rushed and were rushed against each other. I write "were rushed" because of the conscious incitations of their minds. Besides the nationalist rhetoric of the press, the governments of the most advanced democratic states, Britain and the United States, thought it necessary by 1917 to establish large ministries of propaganda (in Britain it was actually called the Ministry of Propaganda, in the United States the Creel Committee). Their publications were full of exaggerations, and often full of outright lies. The present modern use of the word "propaganda," involving the creation of official government departments, originated in 1917. (Nazis and Communists made good use of it thereafter.)

The effects of these publications were regrettable, but also transitory. It took some time until reaction against the wartime propaganda spread wide in Britain and in the United States (that kind of skepticism was to benefit Hitler in the 1930s). Not transitory but enduring were the transformations of entire societies during the war. All kinds of people moved, or were moved, up on the social scale. The war gave an enormous boost to the cause of female equality. Women, again especially in Britain but also in the United States, were now employed in all kinds of occupations and services, in situations unheard of before the war. The cause of women's suffrage was accomplished soon after the war ended; thereafter women not only voted but became Members of Parliament in Britain, congresswomen and in some instances governors of states in the United States. Meanwhile, all over Europe the barriers separating classes became more and more porous; but then wars are almost always powerful, if not always calculated, instruments of social mobility.

Before I go further, a warning: history is never of one piece. During the First World War some conditions of the old order still prevailed. It was a war of vast national armies against vast national armies, but not yet a war against civilians. The civilian populations were increasingly involved in the war efforts of their governments; they suffered and starved during blockades; but they were seldom persecuted or expelled or murdered, except in a few instances. (Such included the, mostly German, first bombing of cities by aircraft; the sinking of merchant and passenger ships; the long-range artillery bombardment of Paris in 1918, etc.) Yet the limitations of warfare between states, something that had begun to spread across Europe about 1650, still existed here and there. There were a few, in retrospect remarkable, episodes of chivalrous or gentlemanly courtesy before, dur-

ing, and after the declarations of war in 1914, especially between states and governments that had not been traditional
enemies. But they were not many—exceptions that prove
the rule, alas.

{"MODERN"?}

L ET US LOOK AT THE STRANGE evolution of the adjective (indeed, of the category) "modern"—letting alone
its more recent, and largely senseless, application to a
noun: "modernization."

"Modern" has two, increasingly disparate, meanings. In
its first (and largely correct) sense it appeared in English
around five hundred years ago. It meant something close to
its original Latin sense, "hodiernus"; in Late Latin: "moder-
nus": current, today's, pertinent. (Shakespeare used it as
"every-day," "ordinary," even "commonplace.") *Ancient and
Modern*: an English, early-seventeenth-century counter-
position of hymns and liturgical texts, appeared a little later.
By the late seventeenth century, due to the emergence of
historical consciousness, "The Modern Age" had become a
great historical category: Ancient-Medieval-Modern, the

three ages of history. Three hundred years later we may criticize this implicit presumption, or at least suggestion: that
The Modern ("today's," "progressing") Age would last forever. Even great historians of Decline and Fall, such as Gib-
bon, failed in not being skeptical about this. Of course so
did almost all thoughtful—or thoughtless—believers in the
idea of progress. We (at least some of us) are older, we know
(or at least we ought to know) more history as we move
along the increasingly uneven avenue of "Progress." We can
see that the past five hundred years constituted a great historical epoch of its own, largely ending now; and whether
we call it the Modern Age or the European Age or the Atlantic Age or the Bourgeois Age matters, as yet, little. In this
(but only in this) sense the hobbling adjective "postmodern" contains some meaning.

  "Modernism," "modernist," "modernize" were additional
verbal outcroppings of the original "modern," applied only
rarely during the eighteenth and nineteenth and early twentieth centuries. But before, during, and then especially after
the First World War, "modern" acquired another meaning—
especially in art, style, fashion, behavior (perhaps even character). With this I am now concerned. "Modern art," whether
in painting or decoration or letters or architecture or music,
burgeoned, spread across the globe in the 1920s. Its applications went much wider than art. "Modern" had become an
approbatory and positive word, especially in the United
States, where "a modern woman," "a modern girl," meant
something close or even identical with "all-American" (while

in Britain and Europe such an application of "modern" could still suggest something faintly critical).

Much, if not all, of this was a reaction to the First World War; but there was more to that. The desire for a kind of revolution, for a breaking away from the bourgeois world, began to move minds well before 1914. "The artist is the antennae of the race," Ezra Pound wrote in 1912, before the war; and then, around 1914, he shouted: "Make it new!" He was right about the first—though only for a short time;* he was wrong about the second. "Make it new"? That was supposed to be the purpose of a revolutionary "newness," of a clean (clean? or, rather, entire) break from the past. In any event, Picasso, etc., preceded the war and the collapse of the old world; but they were only symptoms of a collapse. Cubism and the Vorticists, Satie or Stravinsky, Strindberg or Hamsun, some of them great artists, preceded the war. But the difference, the depth of the distance between, say, Picasso in 1906 and Pissarro in 1902 was (and remains) much greater than that between Pissarro and, say, Delacroix, a century before them.

Yes, the bourgeois world had much to answer for. But so did the haters of what was bourgeois. As so often, the revolutionaries *thought* that they were revolutionaries, that they

* "Though only for a short time": because during the twentieth century the intrusion of publicity confused and compromised what in the past had been authentic in intellectual movements and artistic creations. By now art—or, more accurately: artists—have become inextricably dependent on publicity, on its manipulations of intellectual commerce.

were "new"; but much of that was self-indulgence and, ever so often, an easy way out (consider those "modern" or "abstract" painters who abandoned not only "representation" but the very discipline of drawing). In sum, what most "modern artists" produced was often worse than what was left behind. What was left behind had to be changed, and radically indeed; it could not be merely reconstructed; but what so many "modern" artists and architects and writers made up on top of the ruins has already proved to be not only destructive but ephemeral.

"Modern Art"—it is, largely, over. By and large—there are, of course, exceptions to this—the once positive and attractive sense of "modern" is now passing, mostly because of its ugliness and because of its senselessness. Its forerunners before 1914—Art Nouveau, Sezession, Jugendstil, Gaudí, Frank Lloyd Wright, etc.—are nothing more than period pieces—like someone such as Aubrey Beardsley, perverse and, at least largely, ugly. And—at least largely—senseless too. One example: compare James Joyce's fine writing, in *Dubliners* or *Portrait of an Artist as a Young Man,* with his postwar *Ulysses,* 1922, the still nearly universally accepted icon of Modern Prose Literature. Yet it is *Ulysses* which is a period piece, not the earlier two. Think about this. Modern Art has been, largely, a failure; an episode, a symptom, among other things, of a collapsing civilization. We can see this now, if only we are willing to open our eyes. The 1920s were, really, the *only* Modern decade in the twentieth century. Perhaps especially in music, painting, sculpture, architecture. (Consider, for one, the brilliance and frequent beauty of American popular music then. The turning point came around 1950.) After that: populism and brutality triumphant—at least for a while . . . . It would not last. Proof of this were the 1960s, which were nothing more than loud, crude, artificial and exaggerated imitations, projections of the 1920s. However: their influences became more and more widespread, they involved standards and patterns of living and of building the breaking-up of urbanity, of families, of marriages, the respect for women—the gradual liquidation of an entire civilization now past.

It is a mistake to think that all of these changes were the results of drastic and new material conditions, of the applications of scientific thinking. It was not the invention of photography that brought a change (a good forty or more years later), a change in the vision and then in the methods of great painters. "Impressionism"—proceeding, among other things, from the (not always conscious) recognition that what is seeable is inseparable from the (creative) act of seeing*—was not (or at least less of) a forerunner of "Modern Art" than it was the last shimmering chapter of a great representational tradition, beginning with (and here and there before) the Renaissance, of the Modern Age. It was not the phonograph or the technical reproduction of music that brought about impressionism in music, without

---

*That is: a recognition (again, not always conscious) that a comprehension of the limitations of the human mind may actually enrich it.

which the haunting and brilliant and sophisticated harmonies of modern popular music would have been nothing
but honky-tonk. It was not film, or movies that alone brought
about the deep change which by the middle of the twentieth century affected the very mental processes of millions,
and especially of the young: the reversion from a largely
verbal to a largely (and superficially) pictorial imagination.
Technology contributed to all of this: but that was all.

Look only at the "revolutionary," "radical," "supermodern" posters of the time of the Russian Revolution:
enormous factories with blazing windows, their gigantic
chimneys pumping out billowing clouds of triumphant
promise above great black cities, into the air. They are (and
look) more outdated than any cheap china cup produced
(whether by hands or even by machines) one hundred and
fifty years ago.

THERE WERE, AND ARE, historians who said (and say) that in 1917 the very nature of the First World War had changed. That is both true and untrue. That the United States declared war on Germany in 1917 was decisive, ensuring the victory of the Western democracies a year later. That in 1917 there occurred a Russian revolution (and that Russia then dropped out of the war) was *not* decisive. This requires explanation.

Thousands of historians and political scientists, slews of politicians and even statesmen, the majorities of entire nations and generations have believed, and said, that the Russian Communist Revolution was *the* most important event in the twentieth century—implying thereby that it was even more important than were the two world wars. In 1917, wrote William F. Buckley, Whittaker Chambers, James Burnham, and their "conservative" followers, "history changed gears"—whatever that means. It is nonsense. The Russian revolutions (there were two of them in 1917, a "liberal" and a Bolshevik one) were the consequences of a great European war, not the other way around. The opposite had happened after the French Revolution, in the 1790s. The Bolshevik revolution, unlike the French one, did not spread beyond the Russias. Unlike the French Revolution that flowed into and over the countries of western Europe, a main result of the Communist Russian Revolution was Russia's retreat from Europe, the very shrinking of Russia's domains. Beyond France the French revolutionary armies triumphed and advanced; beyond Russia the Russian revolutionary armies lost and retreated. All of this in spite of—or, perhaps, because?—of the doctrines and the propaganda of the Bolsheviks, which were even more drastic than those of the French one hundred and thirty years before. A comparison of the Enlightenment with Marxism or Leninism is no explanation for this. What mattered was not ideological but national. What happened in Russia was Russian. Russians were Russians, disliked and disrespected by most of the neighbors. Had Communism and Communists achieved power not in Russia but in Germany, the impact of their success across Europe would have been much greater.*

What happened in Russia in 1917 and after was horrible. More people died there in the three years after the war than in the previous three years during it. Entire classes (the bearers of civilization in Russia) were decapitated or exiled. Those were years of mud and ice, smeared and streaked with blood. This is not the place to describe them in any detail.

*Not only because Germans are better organized than Russians but because the prestige of German culture was so much greater (including also peoples and nations who stood on the opposite side from Germany in the First World War).

But this *is* a place to correct an, unfortunately still wide-spread, opinion. The chaotic civil war in the Russias that began in 1918 sputtered out in late 1923, a few sparks of its embers still glowing in the Russian Far East in early 1924. This time frame corresponds with the rule of Lenin, who died in January 1924. There has been a tendency—in myriad books by people who surely ought to have known better—to contrast Lenin (and Trotsky) with Stalin and with what followed (a tendency somewhat less widespread than during the past sixty years but still extant). Yet Lenin (and Trotsky, that erstwhile hero of anti-Stalin intellectuals) were despicable (and not merely deplorable) murderers and rulers, as was Stalin, if not, on occasion, worse. Moreover, compared with Stalin they were fools, without an inkling of statesmanship, without much comprehension of human nature, without the slightest understanding of nationalism—all of these matters that Stalin felt, and learned, and then possessed.

Lenin (and Trotsky) believed that the Communist Revolution in Russia would repeat itself, very soon, perhaps even within a few months, in the former western borderlands of the Russian empire, and then in Germany, of course. The very opposite happened. In Finland, Estonia, Latvia, Lithuania, Poland, first the local Communists and then the Russian Red Army were defeated. Lenin lost about everything (and here and there even more than) the tsars had gained in the west during two hundred years. Local nationalism triumphed over "international" Communism just about everywhere. Much of the same happened south of the Russian empire too, save for the Caucasus. Lenin supported the anti-imperialist dictators of Turkey, Persia, Afghanistan. They accepted his help for a short time and then stamped out their few Communists and pro-Russians. Lenin and his cohorts were left with hopes about China, where then the same process occurred, sooner or later. In 1920 Lenin was supposed to have said that "the road to Paris goes through Peking"—a fool's geography, more foolish even than Hitler's not entirely unreasonable plan twenty years later, when he wanted to get at London via Moscow.* After Lenin died, Trotsky still pretended to believe in International Communism. Stalin did not (more precisely: he learned not to)— which was one, though only one, reason why he was able to get rid of Trotsky.†

The man who gained more from the specter of International Communism than perhaps anyone else was Hitler. This too requires an explanation.

---

*In 1940 and 1941 Hitler believed, and said, that Churchill's Britain had two hopes left: Russia and America. Against America he could do nothing; but once Russia was eliminated, (a) he could be practically unbeatable, and (b) that, and the liquidation of Communism would give many British, and most Americans, doubts whether to continue the war.

†Consider, too—if (against many odds) Trotsky and his kind would have remained at the helm of Soviet Russia, Hitler could have easily fomented a nationalist and anti-Semitic revolution in Russia against Trotsky et al. in the 1930s: a great step, then, toward the German domination of Europe.

Throughout the twentieth century, and surely after 1917, anti-Communism was a dominant political ideology, political tendency, political emotion, political asset. It is wrong to attribute its power and attraction to material motives, to the bourgeoisie's fear, etc. There was an element of fear among anti-Communists; but there was, too, a powerful element of hatred—less among the bourgeois classes than among all kinds of nationalists, including often the lower classes. A history of anti-Communism is yet to be written: an important and massive undertaking that will perhaps never be attempted.

Anti-Communism was, and remains, more than anti-revolutionary. As early as the 1850s such different men as Tocqueville and radical writers in the American South wrote about it.* But its political history must begin in 1917. It was predictable that people in Europe and America would be horrified by the dreadful news coming out of Russia, and by the worrisome symptoms of Communism spreading within or near their own countries. At first the Western Allies were shocked and fearful of Russia's dropping out of the war (and making a peace settlement with the victorious Germans). This led to the limited and, alas, half-hearted Allied

---

*Tocqueville in 1852: "The insane fear of socialism throws the bourgeois headlong into the arms of despotism. . . . But now that the weakness of the Red party has been proved, people will regret the price at which their enemy has been put down." George Fitzhugh in 1854: the enemies of the South were "Communists."

interventions in the Russian civil war. With a little more determination the Bolsheviks could have been crushed in 1918–1919. But after the end of the First World War the governments of western Europe and of the United States recognized that they could not commit their peoples to yet another war in Europe or Russia or Eurasia. Meanwhile, the fear and hatred of Communism went on, fueled of course by the horrid spectacle of what was happening in Russia, and by the—temporary—spectacle of Communist grabs of power in Munich and Budapest. Churchill, for one, argued and fought in vain for more Allied intervention on the side of the anti-Bolshevik forces in Russia. This would not happen. Eventually the existence and the reality of a new Communist-ruled Russian state was acknowledged by all of the great powers, last of them the United States. But powerful emotions and reasonings and attributions, fears and hatreds, went on. Communism and Communists became more than scapegoats; they were, often thoughtlessly and automatically, attributed as the main sources of anything that was evil. There were extreme examples of this in the United States. Perhaps even more telling than some of the events during the first "Red Scare" in 1919–1921 were statements by members of Calvin Coolidge's cabinet—for example by his moderate secretary of state Frank B. Kellogg—to the effect that the troubles in Mexico in the 1920s and in Nicaragua in 1926 were due to "Bolsheviks."

Adolf Hitler understood this only too well. Anti-Communism (much more than anti-Semitism) was the source of his main appeal to conservatives, first in Germany, then abroad. Gradually his appeal appeared among the German working classes too, together with the trappings and the verve and masculine brutality of his nationalism among the young. During the worst years of the depressing economic crisis, the German vote for Communists rose but a few small percentage points, while the National Socialist share of the vote rose from less than 3 percent in 1928 to more than 18 in September 1930 and then to more than 43 in March 1933. Before his ascent to the German chancellorship, Hitler was shrewd enough to emphasize the dangers of Communism. There are innumerable examples of this. In November 1932, for example, he told President Hindenburg that "the Bolshevization of the masses proceeds rapidly," even as he knew that this was not so; he knew that this kind of argument would impress Hindenburg and most German conservatives. Less than three months later they installed him in power. After that his public statements and speeches had the same motto: "The Red revolt could have spread across Germany like wildfire. . . . We have been waging a heroic struggle against the Communist threat." (This at a time when the Communist Party in Germany had been annihilated, its leaders in prison or in exile.) To Germany's Catholic bishops Hitler said: "The defense of Europe against Bolshevism is our task." Abroad, too, any resolution among his potential adversaries to oppose him was undermined by his assertion of anti-Communism; this was, too, one element in Chamberlain's policy of "appeasement." It got Hitler very far. Within the United States, too, the fear of Communism was a prime element among Franklin Roosevelt's opponents during the critical years 1940–1941.* And that anti-Communism was the flag nailed to the mainstaff of the American Republicans, bringing them to power and to the presidency so often after World War II, is only too obvious to detail.

Many books, perhaps entire small libraries, exist about the propagators of and believers in International Communism. That many such existed, and that many of them did at least some harm, is evident. That so many of them, including celebrated intellectuals and artists, would not abandon their beliefs even in the face of evidence of the despicable deeds and lies of the Soviets or of other Communists represented, if not actually incarnated, a sad and widespread human shortcoming: an unwillingness, even more than an inability, to think. What was common in the beliefs of just about all of them, no matter how different they were, was their mistaken view of history—more precisely, of the evolving history of the world. Such a view, at least to some extent, has been shared by myriad other people too who were not necessarily Communist sympathizers: a view which, though badly tattered, remains widespread even now. It is a view inseparable from the general idea of progress, of evo-

*In December 1941, three days before Pearl Harbor, Senator Robert A. Taft proclaimed that while "Fascism" appealed to only a few, Communism was a much greater danger because it appealed to many. (This when Hitler's armies stood a dozen miles from Moscow.)

lution, of democracy, amounting to the progress of mankind; even though this progress may be harmed or compromised by utopians and by their propagation of utopian systems such as Communism, wanting too much and going too fast. Thus such unimpeachably democratic and liberal and non-Communist statesmen as Franklin Roosevelt saw Stalin and his Soviet Russia representing a kind of crude pioneer vision and version of a workers' democracy, as yet unsuitable for Americans and kindred peoples, though still estimable, at least to some extent. Thus Roosevelt saw his United States to be somewhere between Stalin's Russia and Churchill's old Britain. Churchill's vision of history was altogether different. He saw Stalin as a new kind of Russian tsar, ruling a people and a society who were well behind the Western democracies, not ahead of them: a view much more realistic (and historical) than that of Roosevelt and of most Americans at the time.

Of course most people believe and think what they prefer to think and what they want to believe: their vision of the world and their own likes and dislikes, including their fears and hatreds, are seldom separable. There are myriad examples of this, involving nationalism and Communism. (Consider how the great majority of early Communist Party members in the United States were Russian Jews who [and whose parents] had fled from Tsarist Russia; or that the clue to Fidel Castro's "adoption" of Communism and his seeking an alliance with Soviet Russia was his fear and hatred of the United States.)

Therefore we must cast a last, and necessarily cursory, look less at the history than at the psychology of anti-Communism and of anti-Communists. Anti-Communism has been widespread and popular not because it was conservative but because it was nationalist. That the peaks and the most popular appeals of anti-Communism seldom coincided with the greatest threats of approaching Communism is interesting enough; it suggests that anti-Communism was so much more enduring than the Communists' appeal. The highest tides of American anti-Communism (which, lamentably, many Americans at the time equated with American patriotism), the top peaks of American military and nuclear preparations, the greatest burgeonings of the American military-industrial state occurred during the very periods when the Soviet Union was in retreat—in the 1950s during the Eisenhower years, and again in the 1980s during the Reagan years. In the 1980s the Russians gave up their East European empire, their presence in Germany and Berlin, and much of their Communism, not because Reagan forced the Soviet Union into bankruptcy but because people there (including their appointed leaders) hardly believed in Communism any longer—something, with all of its fabulous intelligence apparatus, even the CIA was unable to foresee, as indeed it admitted after the Berlin Wall had toppled. And now consider: in 1945 *many thousands* of Germans committed suicide; some of them not even National Socialist leaders or party members. Yet I know not of a single instance, in or around 1989, when a believing Communist committed suicide because of the collapse of Communism, in Russia or elsewhere. Dogmatic believers in Communism had ceased to exist long before that—even as dogmatic anti-Communists continued to prosper.

Allow me to sketch one last, perhaps speculative but not insubstantial, observation. In one, and not unimportant, sense the Communist revolution in Russia turned out to be a great benefit to the West, or at least to Europe, and certainly to Russia's neighbors. Had Russia stayed in the war only a little longer in 1917, the defeat of Germany would have occurred even earlier than in late 1918. Then Russia, whether semiautocratic or semiliberal, would have been one of the victors of the First World War—cashing in most of the wartime promises that the French and British governments, in secret treaties, had offered in their desperate efforts to keep Russia in the war. What happened at the end of the Second World War, at Yalta, etc., in 1945, would have happened at the end of the First World War: Russia the greatest power in Eastern Europe, the Western Allies in Western Europe, and a weakened Germany in between. Whether Russia could have kept its power and influence over the non-Russian peoples in Eastern Europe remains of course a question. Just as eventually proved after the Second World War, the Russians could not have digested their Eastern European conquests; they were unpopular; their orthodoxy, whether Tsarist or Communist, was especially hateful. At the same time we must consider that in the years before 1914 the conditions of life in Russia were improving: an incipient capitalism had begun to rise, social mobility was slowly increasing, the enormous potential assets of mineral wealth in the Russias was beginning to be exploited; hesitantly, with uneasy, at times faltering, steps, Russia was on her way to something like a pseudocapitalist economy, constitutional monarchy, etc. All of this was swept away by the Communists, with the result that—even despite Russia's victory in the Second World War—Russia fell behind Europe and the West; and so she is still now, for perhaps as many as one hundred years or even more.

{1917 AND THE AMERICANIZATION OF THE WORLD}

B OTH IN THE SHORT RUN (meaning the outcome of the First World War) and in the long run (meaning the history of an entire century) not Russia and not Communism but the United States, with its power, its wealth, its popular influences, was decisive. In the short run, 1917–1918, because with the help of the United States the Western Allies were able to defeat the greatest power in Europe even without Russia—something that they were not able to do against Hitler in the Second World War, and had not been able even against Napoleon more than a century earlier.

In 1917 the crucial event was not the Russian Revolution and not Russia's withdrawal from a European war but America's entry into it. This assured Germany's defeat. But there was more than that. It was the reversal of a world movement of four hundred years. For four hundred years armies and people from Europe (and from Russia) had moved westward across the Atlantic, to America. Now this was reversed. For the first time two million American soldiers were shipped eastward, to help decide a European war. For two hundred years Americans had lauded themselves that theirs was A New World; and that they had and should have little or nothing to do with The Old World and its inhabitants. Now young Americans were going Over There, to teach The Old World a lesson.

That sentiment faded fast; but its essence remained. On the great world scene what happened by 1920 was something no one could have foreseen in 1917. Both Russia and the United States were withdrawing from Europe. For very different reasons of course: the new rulers of Russia were compelled to withdraw, the American people inclined to withdraw. That (in retrospect, somewhat anomalous) situation prevailed for about twenty years—until the summer of 1939 when, again in very different ways and for very different reasons, the shadows of Soviet Russia and of the United States of America reappeared on the European scene. On the level of popular sentiments: by 1920 Americans had

had enough; getting involved in Europe had been a mistake; getting back to "normalcy" (President Harding's verbal invention) was what most Americans really wanted. Moreover (and here the powerful beliefs of anti-Communism played a decisive part), the dominant national wish was now to put an end or at least drastically curtail the immigration of crowds of people from Russia and eastern and southern Europe, potentially or even actually corrupting America and Americanism. That kind of isolationism endured for a while; but it was also superficial. Notwithstanding the Republicans' rule and the nationalism of the 1920s, culturally Paris and Berlin and New York and of course Hollywood were closer in the 1920s than they had been at any time before. And there were Wall Street and Fort Knox: most of the world's gold had now gone to America, and the dollar was the almightiest of the world's monies.

Yet much more enduring than these seemingly (but only seemingly) contradictory movements on different levels of history—and much more enduring than the transitory swing of the Isolationism-Interventionism popular pendulum (the acceptance of the latter in 1917 and its rejection two or three years later)—were the effects of Woodrow Wilson's ideas and their protracted triumph. Since not only the importance of ideas but the very importance of events must be judged by their consequences, let us recognize that the then-great revolution-maker, the effective destroyer of an old order, was Wilson, not Lenin. That Wilson's character was unattractive, that his personality was pallid and cramped, that his mind was immature, that the very workings of that mind were strange, that even the otherwise trenchant observation of his postmaster general ("a man of high ideals but of no principles") was inaccurate, since those very ideas were less than mediocre and customarily superficial—all this is but another example of the irony, even more than of the unpredictability, of history.

"National self-determination" and "Make the world safe for democracy" transformed the history of the twentieth century more than anything else. Another element of irony: revolutionary as the consequences of these Wilsonian proclamations were, they were also old and far from having been original: national self-determination, for one, was an old rusting idea of British Liberalism, going back to Gladstone or even farther. No matter. Just as in 1918 it was not the American Expeditionary Force that turned the tide of the last great battle on the Western front; and yet it was the American military presence in France that decided the war. Ideas and propositions of national self-determination had been current in London and elsewhere before their American proclamation; and yet that Wilsonian proclamation was the decisive push. Wilson and his Progressive cohorts and followers in 1918 believed that this was a war to end all wars; that this was the war between Democracy and Autocracy, that the destruction of the German monarchy meant the historic fulfillment of democracy, that it may have been the greatest event in world history since the coming of Christ. That the world would have been better off with a constitutional monarchy in Germany in 1918, without the destruction of Austria-Hungary, without the creation of such multinational states as Czechoslovakia or Yugoslavia, is at least arguable. What is not arguable is a refutation of the tenet of almost all American liberals and others, that Wilson was a prophet before his time, that had Wilson's League of Nations been accepted by the Senate and by the American people, the Second World War could never have occurred—which is nonsense. And even more important is the fact, or condition, that American foreign policy—indeed, America's view of the world—have remained Wilsonian ever since, adopted by and partaken and believed in by such different men as Herbert Hoover, Franklin Roosevelt, Richard Nixon, George W. Bush.

{THE FAILURE OF LIBERALISM AFTER 1918}

I N THE HISTORY OF THE WORLD not many victories were as short-lived as those of the Western Allies in 1918. They, especially the French, were governed by hatred and fear. Fear soon became the more dominant. The hatred for the Germans soon evaporated among Englishmen (it was never protracted among Americans or even among the French).

Fear of a largely unmutilated, of a sooner or later resurgent Germany sat in Clemenceau's mind and shriveled heart. The results were the botched peace treaties in 1919–1920, especially involving eastern Europe and the Near East. Compared with the Congress of Paris in 1919–1920, the Congress of Vienna in 1814–1815 shines like a sculpture by Canova compared with a sculpture by Epstein. Of course the statesmen at Vienna had been also moved by fear, by their fears of recurrent revolutions in Europe. Soon that did them and their edifice in.

But we have seen that in 1918 and after there was another fear, devolving into hatred—unlike the remnant postwar hatred for Germany that soon began to dissolve. That was the fear and hatred of Communism. And those fears were reciprocal. Lenin and his cohorts and even his successors were obsessed by the fear that the capitalist and imperialist powers were determined to destroy Soviet Russia—which was not the case. One consequence of that fear was their sealing off the Soviet Union from the rest of the world by an "iron curtain": a term that appeared in central Europe twenty-five years before Churchill's famous Iron Curtain speech in Fulton, Missouri, in 1946.

In any event: nothing—or at least very little—of the world before 1914 could be or would be restored. However, that very little included politics. There were no drastic changes in the constitutions of the Western democracies. For a few short years after the war it seemed that the new states and statelets in eastern Europe were establishing par-

liaments on the French or other western European models.
After all, well before the war much of Europe had been
moving in the direction of parliamentarism, liberalism, democracy. But these three matters were not always the same
things. A few years after the war, in many places, it became
glaringly obvious that liberalism, political parties, the very
practice of parliamentary government was inefficient, feeble,
as a matter of fact seemingly obsolete. Among their many
shortcomings there was the condition that the representatives of the existing parties came mostly from the same thin
layers of their societies as they had before: so many bourgeois and lawyers among them. And this was in the 1920s,
after the monstrous earthquake of the war, when such drastic changes in ideas, fashions, behavior, art were taking
place—in America as well as in Europe. This large discrepancy was recognized and trumpeted forth by a few intellectuals; but it was widespread in the atmosphere of those times.

And then, from about 1922 to 1934 in *most* states of Europe (and also in Central and South America) liberal parliamentary governments collapsed and gave way to something more modern (but not "reactionary," as some people
would say). This happened in Italy, Portugal, Spain, Austria,
Poland, Latvia, Lithuania, Estonia, Bulgaria, Yugoslavia, Al-
bania, Turkey, Romania, and then in Germany in 1933—
while boredom, irritation, malaise, dissatisfaction with the
corruptions and hypocrisies of parliamentary politics began
to show evidences in France and even in Britain (and, here
and there, in the United States too). This was, and surely it

seemed to have been, such a general development that in 1930, for a book written by an Austrian (Forst de Battaglia), entitled *Dictatorship on Trial,* Winston Churchill wrote an introduction in which he mused whether this new kind of authoritarianism, while not applicable to the traditional English-speaking democracies, might not be the wave of the future. (About this Adolf Hitler had no doubts—except that authoritarianism was *not* what *he* had in mind.)

It is important to recognize that these mutations, that this decline and sometimes collapse of liberalism, did not necessarily, and often not at all, mean a retreat from democratization. Rather the contrary. Most of the dictatorships or semidictatorships in the countries that abandoned parliamentarism and liberalism decreed and passed laws of social reforms that the preceding liberal regimes had been incapable of. Of course these developments varied from country to country. This is one, perhaps the main, reason why we ought to reject the overall applications of the term "Fascism"—while we ought also recognize that Mussolini's and Hitler's regimes were more modern, more populist (and, at least in more than one sense, more democratic) than those of Lenin and Stalin, but also than their liberal predecessors had been.

{1920 – 1945:
THE DIVISION OF THE WORLD}

THE VERY WIDELY CURRENT PERSPECTIVE of the history of the twentieth century (something almost universally acknowledged by historians) is that the quarter-century 1920–1945 was but a chapter, an episode (albeit an unusual one) of the "main" political history of the century, which was marked by the worldwide contest between Totalitarianism and Democracy. This perspective is wrong, and it must be corrected.

Yes, the twentieth century was a short century, lasting from 1914 to 1989, from the outbreak of the First World War to the collapse of Communist rule in Eastern Europe and then in the Russias themselves. (The nineteenth century was a longer one, lasting ninety-nine years, from Napoleon's fall to 1914, a century that experienced no world wars). But the main feature of the twentieth century was not Communism and not even "totalitarianism." The landscape of this century was dominated by the two enormous mountain ranges of the two world wars, in the shadows of which Europe and America and the world were living until 1989. The Second World War was, in many ways, the consequence of the First

World War, and the so-called Cold War, even more directly, was a consequence of the Second World War. Communist rule in Russia was a consequence of the First World War, Communist rule in Eastern Europe a consequence of the Second.

It could be argued—and it seemed and still seems so to many people, perhaps especially in Britain—that the two world wars in the twentieth century were the last attempt by a state to acquire the domination of most of Europe, this state having been then Germany. There are weighty historical considerations in support of this argument—yet which, even after pondering its essence, is nevertheless insufficient. There are reasons to think that the botched peace settlements of 1919–1920 would and could not have lasted; more important, that a resurgent Germany would and could have risen to become a, if not the, main power in Europe again, about twenty years after Versailles. But: there would not have been a Second World War without Hitler. Not in 1939; not really a world war; and not the kind of war that he brought about. That ought to be reason enough to take him, and his historic role, very seriously. He was the predominant factor of the Second World War—and what preceded it.

During the quarter-century 1920–1945 there were three large forces throughout the world. There was parliamentary democracy, incarnated mostly by the English-speaking nations and the democracies of western and northern Europe. There was Communism, represented and incarnated by the

Soviet Union alone. There was National Socialism and Fascism, incarnated and represented by the German Third
Reich and by Mussolini's Italy. During the Second World
War Fascist Italy collapsed. Yet despite their overwhelming
manpower and industrial might, neither Soviet Russia nor
the English-speaking democracies could have conquered
National Socialist Germany by themselves. The enormous,
and, in many ways, strange alliance of the United States, the
British empire, and Soviet Russia was needed to accomplish that. The military strength and organization of the
German armed forces are not sufficient explanations for
this astonishing condition. Hitler kept the Germans fight-
ing till the very end (and, in most cases, even for a few days
beyond his death).

Unlike during the First World War, during and before
the Second World War the three-way configuration of this
worldwide struggle repeated itself within almost every country. There were Communist minorities in many countries—
though nowhere were they capable of coming to power either by revolutions or with sufficient popular support; until
1945 the Soviet Union remained the only Communist-ruled
country on the globe. There were National Socialist (and,
for a while, Fascist) sympathizers—and, on occasion, near-
majorities—in many countries. There were anti-German
and anti-Fascist and, later, anti-Communist sympathizers
of the Western democracies throughout the world. On occasion their conflicts with their opponents erupted in civil

wars. (These sympathies and antipathies were of course not always separable from the sympathies and antipathies evoked by the protagonist nations representing one or the other of these worldwide forces: Anglophilia and Anglophobia, Germanophilia and Germanophobia were powerful inclinations in many places, as were Russophilia on occasion, and Russophobia on many other occasions.) The universality of this triangular global division appeared well beyond Europe— for example, in China, where at least from 1940 to 1945 three forces struggled with one another: Chiang Kai-shek's Kuomintang, allied with and dependent on the English-speaking democracies; Mao Tse-tung's Communists, allied with and dependent on the Soviet Union; and Wang Ching-wei's nationalists, allied with and dependent on Japan.

In one respect we must qualify this generalization of this triad. There was a fourth, disassociated group of states and governments that were neither Communist nor National Socialist nor liberal-democratic. There existed a diversity of anti-Communist and antiliberal, sometimes semi-parliamentary governments, ranging in the late 1930s from Central and South America to Portugal or Franco's Spain or Greece or the Baltic republics, Austria, Hungary, Romania, Bulgaria, Turkey, and so on. They did not have any attraction beyond their frontiers, and sometimes not even to the majority of the people within them. They may be lumped together under the inaccurate, but perhaps partly useful, designation of "authoritarian"—as indeed it is at least arguable that before 1938 Italian Fascism was authoritarian rather than totalitarian.* Yet many of them—their governments as well as most of their peoples—resisted Germany or Italy or both during the Second World War. Metaxas's Greece was one shining example, but there were others, too, ranging from the cautiously but definitely pro-British course of Salazar's otherwise neutral but surely authoritarian Portugal, to the numerous Central and South American dictatorships or semidictatorships that followed the lead of the United States in 1940–1941 and after. This is yet another reason why the Communist, Leftist, and Russian usage of "Fascist" and "Fascism" were, and remain, not only woefully inaccurate but wholly and historically senseless.

Which brings us to another important consideration. The Second World War (and also what preceded it) was not a war between "Right" and "Left." Hitler—as I suggested before, and as I must insist further—was not a reactionary but a populist. His principal and principled opponents—especially in 1939–1941, when he came so very close to winning his war—were men of the Right, not of the Left: men such as Churchill or De Gaulle. The reputation and the (always partial) popularity of the Left began to rise again only in 1941 and after, pursuant (and not preceding) the military

---

*It is a curious etymological fact that it was Mussolini who in 1926 or 1927 first used the term "totalitarian," meaning the subordination of individualism to the totality of the interests of the national state. But Italian practice did not accord with that meaning, notwithstanding Mussolini's declamatory rhetoric.

successes of the Soviet Union and of Stalin. Many, if not most of the remnant aristocracies and upper classes within Europe were Anglophile, contemptuous of National Socialism and of populism.

Of course there existed collaborationist and opportunist conservatives as well as decent and courageous Socialists* in many countries, including Germany. Yet it was not internationalism or class consciousness but patriotism (yes, often commingled with and inseparable from sentiments of nationalism, despite their essential differences) that furnished the principal resistance to Hitler and Mussolini and to National Socialism. In many places of the world the real division was not between Right and Left but between two Rights. This was so even in the United States, where Franklin Roosevelt's most dangerous adversaries were not on the Left but men such as Huey Long or Father Coughlin in the 1930s and then men such as Charles Lindbergh and many Republicans and former populists by 1940 on the Right. Not that Roosevelt was a man of the "Right"—but that is another story. What we must do first is to dispose of the misused terms "Fascism," and then of "Totalitarianism."

---

*But what George Orwell said so harshly in *The Road to Wigan Pier*, in 1936, had a kernel of unpleasant truth: "One sometimes gets the impression that the mere word 'Socialism' or 'Communism' draw towards them with magnetic force every fruit-juice drinker, nudist, sandal-wearer, sex-maniac, Quaker, 'Nature Cure' quack, pacifist and feminist in England."

{MISUSE AND MISREADING OF "FASCISM"}

THE ADJECTIVE, or category, of "fascist" is still often, and widely, used throughout the world; (a) applied to certain "right-wing" dictatorships; (b) applied to most, or all "right-wing" dictatorships or political parties, including Hitler's Third Reich, during the 1920–1945 period; (c) applied, on occasion, to manifestations of all kinds of authoritarian practices or inclinations. All of these three applications are wrong.

Fascism was largely an Italian phenomenon. Nationalist socialism was more universal. The origins of Fascism were definitely Italian. Those of National Socialism were not purely German. We know that the first appearance of *fasci* as a political grouping arose among agricultural workers in Sicily around 1892. The first appearance of parties named National Socialist arose in German-speaking Moravia and Bohemia a few years later, whereby it may be argued that Fascism preceded National Socialism. This argument is insufficient. Save for the word, the Sicilian "fasci" of the 1890s had nothing to do with Mussolini's *fasci* in 1919 and after. Either in its origins or in its development German National Socialism was not Fascist, whereas eventually Italian Fascism became more and more National Socialist. But before

I come to this development, a word or so about the origin of the overall usage of the "fascist" term in the 1930s and thereafter—since the history of ideas (indeed, of all human thought) is inseparable from the history of words.

Some time around 1931–1932 the usage of the term "National Socialist" was forbidden in Soviet Russia, presumably on Stalin's orders. (This is an important topic that researchers reading Russian might usefully pursue, verify, and complete.) After that date, Russian references to Hitler or to National Socialists or to the Third Reich was always to "Fascists" or "Hitlerites." In western Europe and in the United States this terminology was instantly and eagerly adopted by many journalists and political commentators and even political thinkers and historians—wrongly so. It was the only permissible term employed by all Communists, regimes as well as intellectuals, in the Soviet-dominated nations of eastern Europe.

Stalin had good reasons to insist on this kind of terminology. National, instead of "international" socialism was more and more applicable to Stalin's Russia in the 1930s, whence it was best to avoid the usage of such a term. At the same time the overall application of "Fascism" to all right-wing and strongly anti-Communist parties and practices and phenomena was very useful for international Communist and left-wing rhetoric and practice.

It is regrettable that long after the demise of Mussolini's Fascism and of Hitler's National Socialism, and long after historians' recognition of the not inconsiderable differences between them, not only leftist political writers and thinkers but historians, too, found it proper to employ the overall term of "Fascist" as a common denominator in the senses described in the beginning of this section. A principal example of this was the German historian Ernst Nolte's massive book *Three Faces of Fascism* (1963, 1966), in which he attempted a near-encyclopedic description of three nationalist right-wing movements, the French Action Française, Italian Fascism, and German National Socialism. This book received nearly unanimous approval, even though its thematic concept was entirely wrong. Apart from the sometimes fundamental differences between these three ideologies, Nolte's concept was at least chronologically, that is, historically, incorrect, since the Action Française was essentially a *pre-Fascist*, while Hitler's Third Reich (especially in its later years) was essentially a *post-Fascist* phenomenon—not to speak of the condition that it was the third of these, National Socialism, that eventually had the largest influence on the others and attracted many followers of the other two.

There were differences between Fascism and National Socialism, as there were between Italians and Germans, as there were between Mussolini and Hitler. These differences were historical and national. Again it is history, not theory, that makes them apparent. The relationship between Fascism and National Socialism, between Italy and Germany, between Mussolini and Hitler, had its ups and downs. The low point was 1934, when Mussolini made political (and one or two military) gestures to oppose an eventually abortive Nazi coup in Austria (in essence supporting Austrian "Fascism" against National Socialism), and when Mussolini himself was supposed to have made a few scathing statements against the racist ideas of German National Socialism. Yet even that was neither unequivocal nor definite. Hitler and Mussolini had met a few weeks before the Austrian crisis of July 1934, and their meeting, while inconclusive, was not a failure. Within Italy there were newspaper debates between at least two different Fascist organs, one anti-German and antiracist, the other pro–National Socialist and anti-Semitic. The 1934 crisis (if that was what it was) between Fascist Italy and National Socialist Germany was a glitch, not a break. Very soon it was surpassed, because Mussolini was inclined to see much of the contemporary tendency of Europe as did Hitler, essentially in the light of which both of them were convinced, though in different ways: the decay of the democracies of western Europe, and the consequent weakness of France and Britain (about the latter Mussolini was even more convinced than was Hitler).

There is, however, one important theoretical difference between the political thinking of Mussolini and Hitler, a distinction with consequences. Mussolini believed in the primary importance of the state. The state had to be strengthened, against the endemic individualism of the Italians. In the Fascist manifesto of 1932 Mussolini proclaimed: "It is not the people who make the state but the state that makes the people." He tried to institutionalize and enforce the submission of the individual to the state, harking back, at least in some ways, to the ideal of the state of the Italian Renaissance. But Hitler had already written in *Mein Kampf* that "the state is but a means to an end." And in 1929: "For us the idea of the *Volk* is higher than the ideas of the state." In 1933: "Religions are more stable than forms of states." In 1938: "In the beginning was the *Volk,* and only then came the Reich." In 1944: "The state is only an enforced framework" *(eine Zwangsform).* In 1934, at Nuremberg: "Foreigners may say that the state created us. No! We are 'The State.' We follow the orders of no earthly power but those of God who created the German people! On us depends the state!"

One additional observation about the Fascism–National Socialism relationship, in time and place. In Western Europe the height of the attraction and of the intellectual respect for Fascism occurred in the early 1930s. Thereafter it either ebbed (as in Britain and Ireland, for example), or it began to transform itself more and more into a pro-German or National Socialist direction (as, for example, among the Rexists in Belgium). In Austria the popular dislike of many Austrians for Italy led to the condition that few Austrians were pro-Fascist, while many more of them were pro-German *and* National Socialist. In eastern Europe the populist extreme Right was National Socialist and not Fascist, with practically no exceptions, a tendency in which anti-Semitism

played a definite part. In France the "Right" was Anglophobe and Italophile (and also hispanophile, after Franco's
victory). Spanish Falangism was a more complex phenomenon: it has both Fascist and National Socialist elements,
in particularly Spanish ways. In Norway (and Holland and
elsewhere—for example, Argentina) National Socialist sympathizers were Anglophobes and Germanophiles. In any
event—and well before Mussolini's decision to align himself definitely with Hitler—Fascism had fewer and fewer
admirers and followers across Europe and the world, while
those of National Socialism and Germany were increasing.
All of this took place during the time when the "Fascist"
term was not only bandied about but universally employed,
not only by Russians and Communists but also by all kinds
of Leftists and liberals throughout the world.

After 1945 the survival of Fascist and National Socialist
sympathizers did not essentially alter this condition. It is
National Socialism and not Fascism, it is the Third Reich
and not Mussolini's Italy, that evokes the respective interest
and admiration of such people. In Italy itself, where a neo-
Fascist party has had a now respectably long history, at least
since 1948, the main identification and the ideology of this
party and of its adherents was with Mussolini's Italian Social Republic after 1943 rather than with Mussolini's regime
of the late 1920s and early 1930s. The name was the MSI, the
Italian Social Movement; it extolled Mussolini's decision to
have entered the Second World War and, at least indirectly,

his alliance with Hitler's Third Reich. Le Pen's Front National in France has nothing to do with Fascism: it is nationalist, Anglophobe, and occasionally anti-Semitic, with tendencies of anti-Gaullist Germanophilia, harking back to the Second World War. Jörg Haider's party in Austria shows such tendencies, too—it may be telling that Haider once described Winston Churchill as a "war criminal"—in any case, it has nothing to do with Fascism.

It is senseless to analyze the history of Fascism and of National Socialism apart from Mussolini and Hitler. (At the same time there are German historians, such as Klaus Hildebrand, who have written that there was no National Socialism, there was only Hitlerism. Absolute nonsense.) In one respect Mussolini preceded Hitler. In 1919 Mussolini invented Fascism and founded a new party, whereas Hitler did not invent National Socialism, and in 1919 enrolled in the ranks of a small National Socialist party, though he would soon become its principal personage and leader. Yet, more significantly, Mussolini's own nationalist socialism preceded his Fascism by at least eight years. Around 1911, at the time of the Libyan War, Mussolini realized that, yes, he was a socialist: but a *nationalist* socialist. That marked his career—and the history of Italy, indeed, of Europe—afterward. There followed his famous breakaway from the Italian Socialist

Party in the autumn of 1914. That event, too, was a consequence not only of his earlier conversion to nationalism but
of the fact that when the First World War broke out International Socialism (indeed, Marx's basic dogma of the class
struggle being infinitely more than the struggles of nations;
indeed, the entire idea of Economic Man), sizzled and
melted away in the heat of nationalist emotions.

Dozens of books exist about the relationship of Mussolini and Hitler. What belongs here is nothing more than a
brief summary of the change of their reciprocal situation
in 1938. Before that Hitler admired and respected Mussolini
more than Mussolini respected and admired Hitler. Mussolini was seven years older than Hitler; he came to power
eleven years before Hitler; he was successful and respected
throughout the world. Had it not been for Mussolini, had
Italy been governed by a liberal parliamentary government, it
is questionable whether Hitler, in *Mein Kampf* and thereafter,
would have proposed a German alignment with Italy, and
that Germandom, including Austria, should have accepted
the Italian incorporation of German-speaking South Tyrol.

Mussolini's Italian example also had something to do
with Hitler's decision to come to power not against but with
the help of conservatives. He recognized, too, Mussolini's
Fascist modernity. But in 1938 all of this changed. Before
that Mussolini had been the senior partner in their relationship; in 1938 and thereafter it was Hitler. This had, of course,
much to do with the change in the political map of central

Europe and with the awesome rise of German power. But
there was another element too. During his triumphant visit
to Rome in May 1938, Hitler was disillusioned—indeed,
disgusted—by much that he saw. Italy was, after all, a diarchy: Mussolini ruled with the consent of, indeed together
with, the king. The impression of the bejeweled and corrupt
and fashionable royalty and aristocracy at the Rome recep-
tions upset Hitler. "Fascism is only a half-job," he was supposed to have said earlier. What is not a supposition is there
in his repeated statements excoriating monarchy during
and after his return from Rome. (Among other things, he
privately praised the German Social Democratic leaders for
having gotten rid of the Hohenzollern monarchy in 1918,
and ordered a raise in their pensions.) It was not only that
by 1938 Hitler and his Germany were more powerful than
Mussolini and his Italy: the latter had to accommodate himself to the former. This was evident not only in international
politics but in Mussolini's decision to adopt racism, anti-
Semitism, and other German-inspired measures for Italy
(including the imitation of the German parade march, the
goose step). From then on, with few minor deviations along
the path, Mussolini went downhill, in the end entirely dependent on and even subservient to Hitler.

But this was, again, part and parcel of a larger—and
deeper—phenomenon. After 1938 it was not only that Italy
became subservient to Germany and Mussolini to Hitler:
Fascism had become absorbed by and subservient to National Socialism, nearly everywhere. Even before 1938 there

were many Fascists who became National Socialists; but there were no National Socialists who had become Fascists. The culmination of this was the collapse of the Italian diarchy in 1943, when not only the king but many important Fascists (and not all of them because of sheer opportunism) turned against National Socialism, against Italy's alliance with Germany, and even against Mussolini. Mussolini was arrested, and then rescued by Hitler. The result was the formation of the Italian Social Republic in the north, under German tutelage. In the end Mussolini himself returned to his radical socialist and original republican convictions. A few days before his flight and execution, he turned to one of his followers and said: "If you had a choice what would it be: Italy a British colony, or a Soviet republic? I'd choose the latter." This was useless rhetoric; it was, however, a symptomatic indication of Mussolini's hatreds and fears.

{MISUSE AND MISREADING OF
"TOTALITARIANISM"}

A ND NOW WE MUST DISCARD that stuttering, bumbling, ugly word: "totalitarianism." Its general idea and definition is the total power of a state over its people.* To begin with: such total power, or even control, is not possible, not even in the worst cases of tyrants and tyrannies. Such *total* power over everyday lives does not and cannot exist. It may be argued that such a total, or perfect, condition is not what matters, that what matters is the *purpose* of a dictatorial government to ever extend, to achieve eventually, total control. Yet total control was exercised neither by Mussolini's Fascism nor by Hitler's National Socialism and not even by Stalin's Communism.

We have seen that the "totalitarian" designation was first used by Mussolini in 1926 or 1927, and that there was something operatic about this, melodramatic and surely exaggerated, since Fascism in Italy was and remained less than

---

*According to the *Oxford English Dictionary* (though only in its *Supplement*) it is "a reaction against parliamentarism." This is incorrect, also because many dictators kept parliaments or Reichstags, some of them not even one-party ones.

total. But even a distinction between Mussolini's "authoritarian" and Hitler's "totalitarian" dictatorship will not lead us far—in part because Hitler's regime, too, was not really "totalitarian." He never used this word;* but, then neither did most Germans think that they were deprived of many (let alone all) of their freedoms while living in the Third Reich.† This is not a defense or even a mitigation of the brutal realities of Hitler and of National Socialism. My purpose is to direct attention to the inaccurate, or worse, misleading, use of the "totalitarian" word.

The term appeared here and there before and during the Second World War, when it was applied mostly to Germany and to its allies. For many kinds of ideological and personal reasons many people did not apply it to Soviet Russia and Communism (selective indignation being a main component of political preferences and of ideological thinking). Again we ought to recognize a principal shortcoming of the liberal vision of political history, inherent in the

*His chief propagandist Goebbels, too, used it only on occasion: that is, in his famous speech after the catastrophe of Stalingrad in February 1943, when he incited his audience to shout their approval of "Total War."

†Even the term "dictatorship" is not entirely applicable to Hitler's Third Reich. Hitler himself said on one occasion that he was not a dictator: "Every South American popinjay can be a dictator." He was something more frightening and more powerful than a mere tyrant—and the establishment of his rule had been supported by the majority of the German people. As the moderate and modest Ian Kershaw put it: "To suggest that Hitler's power rested on 'totalitarian terror'—leaving aside difficulties with the concept of 'totalitarian'—is to state only a partial truth."

minds of many thinkers and writers, for whom "totalitarianism" and particularly its "extreme Rightist" versions are "reactionary."

When, then, after 1945, the brutalities of Stalin's Soviet Russian and of other Communist dictatorships became more and more evident to public knowledge in the West, the political and ideological semantics simplified. "Totalitarianism," the tyranny of state control, the police state, ideological censorship, etc., they were much the same thing. For nationalists, especially in the United States (many of them later discovering that they were "conservatives"), Communism was the worst existing and imaginable tyranny of all, much worse than Fascism or National Socialism, than Hitler or Mussolini (and of course than Franco); and to them the most contemptible were Communism's liberal fellow-travelers, allies and dupes of Stalin during the Second World War (sometimes they included Roosevelt and Churchill among the latter). We must not underestimate the influence of this kind of nationalist anti-Communist vision of the world, an ideology which became more than an ingredient, indeed an equivalent, of American patriotism, and which carried its proponents far.

Alas, similarly enduring (among intellectuals at least) was the theory of totalitarianism produced by Hannah Arendt, a muddled and dishonest writer, in a book, *The Origins of Totalitarianism*, that appeared at a most propitious moment, in New York, in 1951. (A most propitious moment: since that was the very time when an entire generation of American leftist intellectuals and academics were abandoning their illusions about Communism and Stalin.) Her book had two theses. First, that anti-Semitism was the ingredient of every totalitarian regime—which was, and remains, nonsense. Second, more important: that it was and is in the very nature of totalitarian regimes to increase their terror, to extend their rules deeper and deeper and further and further, among their peoples and across the world. Less than two years after the publication of *The Origins of Totalitarianism* Stalin died and the reduction of police terror within the Soviet Union began. Another three years later the Polish and Hungarian revolts against Communism broke out. No matter: the reputation of this "seminal" work and of its author rose and rose (among other things, institutes and an express train became adorned by her name in Germany). Her adulation among American intellectuals persists to this day.*

Freedom and freedoms; restrictions of freedoms, the wish—or appetite—for freedom, indifference to freedoms—these are difficult and problematic matters, and perhaps especially during the democratic epoch. To regard freedom

---

*A summary about the dishonest origins of *Origins . . .* is relevant. Arendt's original, and hardly readable, manuscript was "completed" in 1946–1947 and dealt only with Nazism. Laden with interminable references and quotes from a spate of obscure books by other refugee authors, it was bandied about among various publishers in New York who rejected it. Then, hurriedly, in 1948–1949, she added two chapters about Stalin's Communism. The footnotes of her "research" reveal that she had read a total of three books about *that* subject.

simply as an emancipation from chains, as an absence of restrictions is of course insufficient. Aristotle knew that it is
more difficult to be free than not to be free. That political
freedom does not exhaust the meaning of freedom ought
also be obvious. (At the time of Mussolini's proclamation of
"totalitarian," 1926: was not the life of an American visitor
freer in Italy than in his native state—considering Prohibition, among other things?) Already Tocqueville noted something related to The Tyranny of the Majority: that a man in
the United States may be free to express his personal opinions but that against the massive power of "public opinion"
(let alone popular sentiment) he was helpless, condemned
to a kind of loneliness that was worse than solitude. Considerable leeways and even liberties in personal, economic,
intellectual, etc., lives existed or continued to exist not only
in Mussolini's Italy but in Hitler's Third Reich.* What these
dictatorships would not permit, what they were principally
concerned about, was actual and here and there potential
opposition to them, evident in public. In this respect, but
in this respect only, there was no great difference between
these police states in the twentieth century and many absolutist regimes in the more distant past. The great difference

*The extent of intellectual freedoms (including that of occasional
publications) in these states was considerable; a study of them is still
wanting. It may even be argued that after Stalin the Soviet Union (and,
after 1956, some of the Communist satellite countries of Eastern Europe)
were no longer "totalitarian" but "authoritarian." That would be a semantic argument; more important is the question how much (if any) of
these intellectual liberties matter in mass societies.

was that of populism: the support of such dictatorial governments (at worst) or the indifference (at best) to them by the mass of their peoples—almost always because of their nationalism.

{MISUSE AND MISREADING OF NATIONAL SOCIALISM AS AN "IDEOLOGY"}

L ET ME RETURN—for the last time—to Hitler, whose nationalism was a more important factor of his people's loyalty to him than were the various social improvements and institutions of the Third Reich.

Nationalism in Germany (as also elsewhere) was a substitute of religion for some. What is more significant—and worrisome—is how nationalism, including Hitlerian nationalism, coexisted with religion in the minds of many people; and in that coexistence their nationalism was, ever so often, stronger and even deeper than was their religion. I read an admission of this in a serious Englishwoman's words to a women's club in 1941. She said: "We have a need of a religious faith as powerful as the German people's belief in Hitler."

For Hitler art, too, was inseparable from nationality. "True art is and remains eternal," he said, and added: "It does not follow the law of fashion; its effect is that of a revelation arising from the depths of the essential character of a people." (Yes and no: for what is the "essential" character of a people?) However, my topic is not Hitler but the phenomenon of his appeal and of his power. It was the impression and the accumulated reputation of his power, rather than the ideology of National Socialism, that mattered. This is why a detailed and precise analysis of National Socialist ideology does not matter much. A startling example of this is the German people's reaction to the surprising news of the German-Russian or Nazi-Soviet or Hitler-Stalin pact in August 1939. We have seen how and why Hitler was able to bring the great majority of German conservatives to his side, and how his popularity and prestige profited from the strident assertions of his anti-Communism, that National Socialism represented the very antithesis of Communism. Yet we know of not a single instance of a National Socialist or of a German nationalist conservative tearing up his party card or expressing his shock and disillusionment at the Führer's pact with Stalin. To the contrary: millions of Germans saw that as but another instance of Hitler's genial statesmanship.

Ideology mattered less and less. The unknown English wag who was supposed to have said in August 1939 that "All the Isms are Wasms" was more right than wrong. Ideological commitment meant of course much to intellectuals and others: there were thousands of Communist or pro-Communist intellectuals in the West whose disillusionment with Communism started in August 1939. (That they were, after all, only a small minority among Communists worldwide is but one proof of the melancholy human condition: the unwillingness of most people to change their minds, even within the sight of clear and definite evidence.) It also means that National Socialists were tougher and tougher-minded than were most Communist and pro-Communist intellectuals.

And of course Stalin was no ideologue either. Despite having been born in Georgia, he was a Russian nationalist. Evidences for this are myriad and multiform. His hatred and expulsion of Trotsky, his liquidation of many of the International Communists in the purges of the 1930s were stark and early proofs of his inclinations—indeed, of his convictions. There are many, many evidences of his nationalism—conveniently ignored by the lately so industrious anti-Communist intellectuality. Two trenchant examples. As early as 1934, but then again in July 1940, an article by Marx's friend and patron Engels, "On the Foreign Policy of Russian Tsarism," was about to be published in a leading Russian Communist journal, *Bolshevik*. Andrei Zhdanov, already suspecting Stalin's inclinations, thought it necessary to submit it to him. Stalin's written notes were: "Aggressive vileness is not a monopoly of Russian tsars." "In attacking Tsarist foreign policy, [Engels] resolved to deprive it of any trust." In April 1941 he told Georgi Dimitrov, the head of the Communist International: "The International was formed in Marx's time in the expectation of imminent international revolution. The Comintern, too, was formed in such a period in Lenin's time. Today the *national* tasks of the various countries have priority. . . . Do not cling to what was the rule *yesterday.* Take strict account of the new conditions that have arisen." We ought to recognize that Stalin's termination of the Comintern in 1943, his substitution of a Soviet Russian national anthem for the "Internationale" around the same time, his easy propagation of nationalist themes, his adoption of the names of Kutusov, Suvorov, Bagration for high military medals or for the code names of military operations, his restoration of other Russian traditional military symbols, his support of the Russian Orthodox church hierarchy, etc., were not tricks to mislead or to impress his allies; nor were they altogether opportunist measures to nourish his popularity among masses of Russians but genuine examples of his increasingly nationalist ideology. (In his single speech after the victory in Europe, in June 1945, he praised the Russian people, without saying a word about Communism, or about the Party.)

But more is involved here than the recognition that Stalin—like Hitler or Mussolini or many other dictators— was a nationalist. There was a fundamental difference between Stalin and Hitler (as there was one, too, between

Hitler and Mussolini though of much lesser importance). Even before the emergence of his nationalist consciousness, Stalin recognized (unlike Trotsky, but also unlike Lenin) the importance—nay, the priority—of the state. This of course was but one source of his early confrontation with Trotsky, when Stalin recognized the—obvious—priority of the Soviet Union ("Socialism in One Country") over the propagation of International Communism. Another, perhaps more telling, evidence exists in a telegram that Stalin sent to Orzhonikidze as early as in September 1931. He criticized the Central Committee and the Politburo, and especially Kaganovich (the Jewish member of the Politburo who was close to him but from whom he gradually distanced himself during the 1930s, even though Kaganovich remained the only Jew in the Politburo till the end). Stalin wrote: "What is better: putting pressure on the state's reserves of foreign currency while preserving the peace of mind of the economic apparatus, or putting pressure on the economic apparatus while preserving the interests of the state? I think the latter is better than the former."

"The interests of the state." Stalin's mind was developing. This, among other things, may be a general and overwhelming (though of course neither simple or perfect) explanation of Stalin's 1936–1939 purges, with the result of a large-scale transformation of a party bureaucracy to a state bureaucracy. One outcome of this was his—pragmatic—1939 pact with Hitler. Beyond (and beneath) this, Hitler's in-

fluence on Stalin (and of National Socialism on Communism) was considerable. Hitler respected and even admired
Stalin, and there exist ample evidences of Stalin's respect for
Hitler too. But what is relevant to my argument is not so
much Stalin's respect for German power or his appreciation
of the institutions that Hitler made: this is not the place to
list evidences and the evolution of clandestine Nazi-Soviet
relations or for a comparison of German and Soviet police
rule, including those of their prison camps. What belongs
here is the question: Were Stalin's ideas ahead of Hitler's?
Were they more "modern"? To many intellectuals, and also
to other people, it seemed that Communism was a wave of
the future. Yet in 1945 and afterward Stalin felt constrained
to depend on the installation of Communists in his new
satellite empire, many of them men and women whom he
despised, while he thought that they were about the only
ones who would unreservedly obey him. This had not been
so with Hitler. "The state," originally anathema not only to
Marx but also to Lenin, had become sacrosanct in Stalin's
Soviet Union by 1939, in official terminology as well as in reality. Thus Stalin realized the supreme importance of the
state at the very time when Hitler found that supreme importance to be antiquated, when comparing it with that of
the nation: another example of the backwardness of Stalin's
Communism compared with Hitler's National Socialism.

The primacy of nationalism in the different compounds
of nationalism and socialism survived Hitler. Less than six

months after his death a nationalist-socialist regime came to power in Argentina, led by Perón; and thirty or more years later, toward the end of the sordid self-liquidation of "International" Communism (international in hardly more than a name), the last Communist tyrants discovered, and for a while successfully used, the appeals of nationalism. Ceauşescu in Romania and Milosevic in Serbia, and also others of their kind, were nationalist Communists—again with the definite emphasis on the first of the two categories, often to the extent of nearly eliminating the second. By the end of the twentieth century they too had disappeared. And yet the question may be raised: while Stalin survived Mussolini and Hitler, will the remnant appeal of Communism survive the historical, or nostalgic, appeals of Fascism (in Italy) and of Nationalist Socialisms (not only in Germany and Austria but elsewhere too in the world)?

"The kernel of the phenomenon of Hitler was a fundamental underestimation of [the attraction of] National Socialism"—that is, not only of Hitler but of the ideas he seemed to represent and incarnate—wrote an eminent German historian, Karl-Dietrich Bracher. Or consider the corresponding (and perhaps ominous) statement by another German historian, Hagen Schulze, buried within the dialogue of the deaf that was the *Historikerstreit,* the Historians' Controversy, in 1986–1987, about that important experience "in our [German] history: that the constitutionalists of the first German [Weimar] republic had nothing effec-

tive to counter the enormous national appeal of the nationalists. Certainly the experience of the Third Reich has considerably dampened the German inclination to nationalist extremes"—but it is questionable "whether the kind of
dampening will last more than one or two generations, despite all of the political pedagogy about the efficiency of
which one should have no illusions."

Nor should we have illusions about the permanence of
the constitutional validity of the laws according to which in
Germany, as in Austria, the display of swastikas and of pictures of Hitler remain forbidden, nearly sixty years after his
demise. Red flags and Communist symbols are not forbidden; Nazi ones are. Lenin's or Mao's works can be printed
and published; *Mein Kampf* cannot. We must hope that
when the time for the abandonment of such proscriptions
arrives, such a legal ruling will reflect a climate in which the
symbols of Hitler's era will attract nothing more than historical curiosity.

But that is still in the future. Meanwhile, we ought to
consider the tendency of journalists and of political commentators throughout the Western world: their extreme
sensitivity to every manifestation suggesting the appearance
of so-called right-wing political phenomena anywhere. That
sensitivity is not comparable to anxieties about a resurgence
of the extreme Left. It is not attributable to "political cor-
rectness" (a stupid phrase) either. It reflects, instead, anxiety
and fear about the potential mass appeal of populist nationalism in the age of popular sovereignty.

During the historical (1815–1914) nineteenth century both the history and the political structures of the United States and of Europe differed greatly. The main events in the history of Europe were the revolutions of the 1820s, 1830s, and 1848, and thereafter the unifications of Italy and of Germany. In the history of the United States they were the westward movement, the Civil War, and mass immigration. In most of Europe the political history of that century was marked by the debate between conservatism and liberalism; in the United States, where no conservative party or movement existed, it was not. During the twentieth century these divergences ceased to exist. Both for Europe and the United States the two great mountain ranges that characterized the century were the two world wars, and then the so-called Cold War, which was a consequence of the Second World War. Moreover, after about 1955, for the first time a self-designated "conservative" movement emerged in the United States; and a quarter-century later more Americans identified themselves as "conservatives" than as "liberals." But this was only part and parcel of a wider and deeper development, obscured though it has been by the traditional terminology of American politics. As in Europe, and also as elsewhere in the world, the predominance of nationalism and socialism has governed American politics during the entire century. Save for some details, the welfare institutions and practices of American government do not essentially differ from those of other democratic and so-called "advanced" nations; and, all political rhetoric notwithstanding, these measures are accepted by the great majority of the American people and also by their two large political parties. Meanwhile, the United States has not been immune to the stronger appeal of nationalism than of socialism; and as I wrote earlier, while the Republicans tend to be more nationalist than socialist, the Democrats tend to be more socialist than nationalist. This has been so for three generations, eighty or ninety years at least. Some time in the future this may change: but not yet.

It is because of its nationalism that the Republican Party has become populist, at least during the past forty or so years. We have seen that by the 1930s American progressives and populists diverged: most of the remaining progressives became internationalists, while most of the populists were nationalists. Indeed, it may be argued (and the United States is but one example of this widespread phenomenon) that, more than often, populism *is* nationalist socialism. And while populists remain opposed to international capitalism, they have become less and less inimical to nationalist capitalists or to nationalist billionaires. But of course what are still called "capitalism" and "capitalist" in 2000 have become something entirely different from capitalism and capitalists in the nineteenth century. A good thorough cleansing of the basic language of economics is even more overdue than a rethinking of certain accustomed and antiquated categories of politics. But that is another story.

{THE UNITED STATES IN 1945 AND THEREAFTER}

IN 1945 Hitler and Mussolini were gone, Stalin less than eight years thereafter. The United States was on the top of the world. And the Americanization of the world leaped forward, soon in full swing.

An interesting question arises. When was America at its zenith? 1918, or 1945, or 1989? In 1918 the United States did not have to share the victory with Russia. (It had to be shared with Britain and France but this mattered not much: what mattered was the desire of the American people to withdraw from Europe, for twenty years, while the Americanization of mass culture went on.) In 1945 the United States had to share the victory with Russia: they divided Europe, including Germany, and a portion of the Far East among themselves. After 1918 the dollar, and Wall Street, had replaced the earlier primacy of the British pound sterling and of London. But in 1945 there was more to that primacy: the dollar was at its empyrean peak, all-powerful, and the American navy alone was larger than the navies of almost all of the rest of the world combined. And what happened in 1989 was unique in the history of the world: the second-greatest world power, the Soviet Union, gave up the global struggle, it retreated from Europe and from Germany without really having been forced to do so, and the Russian people accepted this without much of a murmur. So there came to be but one Superpower in the world, the United States—an event with enormous and unforeseeable consequences.

But it was (and remains) not as simple as that. *Manhattan 1945* is the title, and the subject, of a telling book by the intelligent and insightful British (Welsh) writer Jan Morris, reminiscing about how wondrous New York was then, pulsating with life, vigorous, sparkling, at the top of "everything." Forty years later all, or almost all, was different. *Manhattan 1945* remains a small attractive canvas, saturated with impressionist colors of nostalgia, but Jan Morris (for once) missed something about that democratic vista. There was (and is) Tocqueville's great maxim: that while the prime sin of aristocratic ages was that of pride, that of the democratic age is that of envy. Jan Morris missed what was going on under the surface of all of that buoyant American optimism and confidence. And envy is but one, though widespread, democratic manifestation of the hidden existence of hatreds and of fears.

One of the manifestations of the latter was American anti-Communism, *the* popular substitute for patriotism. Another matter, less visible but sometimes palpable, was the coexistence of an exaggerated American optimism with an exaggerated American pessimism, within American souls and minds. What Joseph Conrad once wrote about Russians in *Under Western Eyes*—"a terrible corroding simplicity in which mystic phrases clothe a naive and hopeless cynicism"— applies, alas, to many Americans too. After all, hadn't Lincoln said of America: "The last best hope of mankind"? The last? Meaning that mankind would soon be doomed to extinction? And this to a people obsessed with Progress and Evolution? Was—is—America the pinnacle of mankind's destiny? Even forty years before Lincoln, John Quincy Adams (the same wise Adams who said that the United States does—i.e., should—not go abroad in search of monsters to destroy) said in the same speech, in 1821: the United States, "A City upon a Hill": "A beacon on the summit of mountains to which all the inhabitants of the earth may turn their eyes for a genial and saving light till time shall be lost to eternity, and the globe itself dissolves, nor leave a wreck behind." There is something strangely unhistorical and profoundly pessimistic in this vision. And disturbing: for the fate of mankind indeed seems catastrophic if Americans do not free themselves from the thought that they are *the* last hope of earth. And especially in a disaster-bound nuclear and technological age, where many Americans, at least in their imagination, like to think of men and women advancing out of the earth into, "Space."

There are innumerable examples of this kind of thinking. The imperialist Albert J. Beveridge in 1900: "God has made us the master-organizers of this world." The Catholic Archbishop Dennis O'Connell in 1898: "Now God passes the banner to the hands of America, to bear it. . . . America is God's apostle in modern times. . . . War is often God's way of moving things onward . . . the survival of the fittest." Such were the words not of an Anglo-Saxon imperialist, not of a Protestant warrior, not of a social Darwinist, but of a fairly "liberal" Irish-American archbishop. Or Michael Novak, a Catholic "conservative" publicist in 1983: "The American people are, by every test of fact, the most religious on this planet." By every test of fact? Did these men believe what they were saying? I think yes. Their view of America and of the world was of course superficial. But in the age of democracy what is superficial often matters, because of the very nature of society, of the structure of events, of the widespread extent and propagation of such slogans at the expense of private thinking and of self-knowledge.

That the United States had become the main power in the world in 1945 was, as a matter of course, a boon for the large part of mankind. There were really no alternatives. Had the United States withdrawn from most of Europe and the Far

East, the extension of the Soviet Union and the spread of Communism may have gone further—though it may have been even less enduring in the long run than what was to happen in Eastern Europe before and in 1989. (The British were not to be counted upon, exhausted as they were materially and mentally. In 1945 they could have assumed the leadership of much of western and northern Europe, as I once wrote: for a song. None of them gave this even a flicker of thought.)

Consider that, at least in Western Europe, the reaction to the Second World War and the results of the Anglo-American victory in 1945 was conservative (in the best sense of this now much abused and perverted word). The queen of Holland, the king of Norway, the grand duchess of Luxembourg returned to their countries, surrounded by universal jubilation. The king of Denmark, virtual prisoner of the Germans, was adored and feted by his people (including Danish Communists). The parliaments of Western Europe's nations were resuming their functions. Labour won the election in Britain, but that, too, was a repudiation of the Tories, not of Churchill. There was a surge of Communist voters in France, Italy, Belgium and the expectable affiliation with Communism among intellectuals and opportunists, but this did not matter much. The conservative reaction to the Second World War went deeper than that, especially in Germany, something that was attributable to more than the fear of Communism. It was a natural reaction against Hitlerism, against the police state, and other

restrictions. That was exemplified by the West German constitution, and by the economic liberalism instituted by Ade-
nauer and Erhard.* It is to the credit of the United States
that it supported these developments (without quite recog-
nizing their conservative essence). The Marshall Plan, and
NATO, meaning the permanent stationing of American forces
in western and southern Europe, and the first peacetime
military alliance of the United States with European states,
were consequences of this.

There was also more—much more—to this presence
of American influences in the world. In some countries
there developed something akin (though of course not
identical) to the party systems of the English-speaking democracies: a turn away from the former impracticabilities
and shortcomings of proportional representation with its
many parties, toward a two- or three-party system. Much
more important, and enduring, was the extension of the democratization of entire societies: the gradual adoption of
the American practice of giving credit to the masses. This
went beneath and beyond politics. The advantages emerged
of income over capital, of creditability over actual property:
they replaced the older, more or less strict capitalist phe-

---

*In 1946 the Republicans won in the congressional elections, helped
by the suggestive slogan: "Had Enough?" That was a—yet unspoken—
reaction against Roosevelt and the Second World War and his alliances
with Britain and the Soviet Union: less honest and, at least potentially,
more disturbing than the reactions of most Germans, who truly had had
enough of dictatorship and of the catastrophe it had brought.

nomenon, expressed by the French aphorism "On ne prête qu'aux riches"—one has to be rich to be able to borrow. The result was a rise of mass prosperity (though conditioned by constant inflation); and the consequent weakening—indeed, lack of interest—in radical or revolutionary political impulses, something that Tocqueville had foreseen. In sum: 1945—of course outside Eastern Europe—was a triumph of democracy and of liberalism, though the former was more important than the latter.

There was, of course, anti-Communism. We have seen that in the United States it became, latest by 1947–1948, a substitute (and often even more than a substitute) for old-fashioned patriotism. It was but another outburst of nationalism, with its appreciable and sometimes dominant elements of fear and hatred. The prewar isolationists had become extreme interventionists. But leaving aside the psychic and mental components of anti-Communism, we may as well notice that it was marked by a misreading of the world after 1945. The—well-justified—American concern should have been with Russian power, not with Communist ideology. Eastern Europe and East Germany, which fell to the eastern side of the Iron Curtain (with tacit American agreement—indeed, with acquiescence in 1945 and after), had Communist governments not because of the popular appeal of Communism but because Russian armed presence had imposed them. Throughout the entire so-called Cold War this remained so, for more than forty years. There was not one western or southern European country that became, or even tended to become, Communist. After 1945 the United States feared that International Communism, having been installed in Eastern Europe, would now spread westward. This was not the case. (Even Stalin did not want that, for more than one reason.) On the other hand, Stalin and the Russians feared that the United States, having established its influence and presence easily in western and southern Europe, might try to uproot or destroy the Russian sphere of influence in Eastern Europe, which also was not the case. That division of Europe (and of much of the world) continued as a reality. In 1962 Moscow (all of International Communist fraternity notwithstanding) had not the slightest intention of risking an atomic war with the United States because of Cuba; in 1956 the United States (all of its anti-Communist "liberation" propaganda notwithstanding) had not the slightest intention of intervening in Hungary during and after its revolt against the Soviet Union. Besides, the Soviet Union was in retreat even well before 1956. In 1948 Yugoslavia broke away from Russian domination. In 1953 came revolts in Poland, East Germany, and in 1956 again in Poland and in Hungary. In 1953 Moscow even contemplated for a while the abandoning of the Communist government in Eastern Germany in exchange for some kind of an American withdrawal from West Germany. In 1954– 1955 Moscow gave up its military and naval bases in Finland and China, and made up with Tito's Yugoslavia. It withdraw from Austria, which was more than a remarkable concession; and it gave official recognition to West Germany without demanding that America and the Western Powers extend such a recognition to Communist East Germany. What then happened, after 1960, in Cuba or Nicaragua or Indochina, were not internationalist but nationalist Communist assumptions of power. Yet throughout the Cold War the American—governmental as well as popular—view of the world was not pragmatic but ideological.

Within the United States this had enduring consequences. "Conservatism" in America was inseparable from anti-Communism (and also from antiliberalism). By 1981 it brought Ronald Reagan to power; and it did not disappear or weaken after the collapse of the Soviet Union either—in many ways, rather the contrary.

I put "conservatism" within quotation marks—because there was (and still is) so much in American "conservatism" that was (and is) not conservative at all. Plainly, the United States was not a conservative influence in the world during the past sixty years. Well before the revolutionary (or, more accurately: fake-revolutionary) 1960s there was nothing conservative in American mass entertainments, in American art, in American literature (well, save for a few eccentric and valuable exceptions), in the American cult of youth, in American rock music, in American films, in American manners, in American behavior, in the sexual and racial changes that actually preceded 1960, during what thoughtless historians and political scientists still describe as the "stuffy" Eisenhower decade. Thereafter the "revolutionaries" of the 1960s were merely playing at "revolution" (just as many of the American Communists in the 1930s, too, enjoyed playing at spying). That play element—*Americanus homo ludens*—existed on other levels, too, as with Ronald Reagan, who enjoyed playing the role of president, or George W. Bush, who enjoyed playing soldier. Here was the duality of the American character: stunning transformations of personal and sexual and civilizational behavior, involving the dissolution of families, including millions of people who identify and see themselves as "conservatives."

That was (and remains) more than a passing phase, more than an ephemeral phenomenon. History does not move like a pendulum. There was no return to the (no matter how superficial) manners, morals, mores before 1950. To the contrary: by about 1980 there was no overall or even significant difference in the personal behavior (including sexual habits) of liberals and conservatives, Democrats and Republicans, urban and suburban populations. The extant dualities were often paradoxical: permissiveness together with the admiration of crude power; a superficial propagation of privacy together with the widespread weakening of private moral standards and convictions, the celebration of legal ownership and of personal property at the same time when in reality people were not owners but renters; the disappearance of most of the former and privately known differences of class together with the unceasing appetite for publicly demonstrable labels of "class." More and more people insisted that the legal (and sacramental) institution of marriage be properly extended to them—at the same time when family life and family ties were fraying and often disappearing. Even more essential was the paradoxical duality involving the relations of men and women: the previous, private and public, legal and social restrictions of women ceased while at the same time the customary respect due to women was vanishing. "A society that places no value at all on chastity will not place much value on fidelity either," an excellent maxim by an Englishman (Theodore Dalrymple). Meanwhile the mutations in manners, morals, mores spread from America worldwide.

It was a roiling and mobile civilization marked by a steady increase in carnality, vulgarity, brutality. Yet, oddly, the institutions and the accustomed frameworks of liberal parliamentary democracy, of that highest creation of the now passing Modern Age, continued to exist—at a time when civilization itself (a term first appearing in English in 1601) was coming apart. History is not governed by logic: but we must at least consider that this strange duality cannot exist much longer: that sooner or later the very political structure of democracy may undergo a deep-going and at least for a while irreversible transformation, including mutations that may have already begun.

{THE DECLINE OF THE STATE}

T
O COMPREHEND THESE MUTATIONS we must take a good hard look at the state of The State.

No comprehensive history exists of the modern state (except perhaps of its beginnings). The state, as we know it, began to emerge in the Italies, in the fifteenth century. Its modern—present—use in England and English appeared first during the sixteenth century. It suggested progress after the frequent disorders and near-anarchy at the end of the Middle Ages. It was inseparable from the increasing power of kings. The absolutist (a better word than "absolute") authority of monarchs reached its peak not in the Middle Ages but in the late sixteenth and seventeenth centuries. This alone refutes the democratic and liberal idea of "progress," since at least in Europe "progress" was not from monarchy through aristocracy to democracy but from aristocracy to monarchy and thereafter to democracy. In most countries the power of the kings was supported by the rising nonaristocratic middle classes. But then, a century or more later, the growing middle classes, the erstwhile beneficiaries and supporters of the monarchs' power, became fretful, rising against the increasingly cumbrous and perhaps even antiquated powers and institutions of monarchs around whom, by that time, stood aristocracies, many of them created by the later kings.* This was of course what happened in seventeenth-century England, and in eighteenth-century France and America (though not in similar ways)—which is why we ought to take a last look at the changing relationships of the monarchs and states.

The monarch needed support—material support—for himself and for the state, for the safety and well-being of both. For safety: the existence and the financing of armies and navies depended on the king and on his revenues. For his and for his country's well-being: his court's upkeep, together with a host of other expenditures that he had to provide, with the help of tax revenues. He and the royal household were often in debt: the state finances sometimes less so. In addition—or, perhaps, even more important—the existence of kingship or of queenship was another element of security for the country and for its people. The monarch was their patriarch, the august head of a family. The hereditary practice and principle merely safeguarded this secure sentiment of continuity: a good monarch may have a bad son, but, still. . . . The old belief that there was some kind of a divine essence in a monarch faded in the seventeenth and

---

*Before that, mostly during the seventeenth century but in other places during the eighteenth, aristocracies were often, though not everywhere, inimical to the central powers of their monarchs—indeed they were "republicans"—but they lost.

eighteenth centuries (save for occasional reaffirmations at significant ceremonies), but the sense (if not always the essence) of royal authority prevailed, for a while unimpaired by publicity. During the nineteenth century, and with the spreading of constitutional monarchies, the importance and often the example (consider Victoria or even Franz Joseph) of this parental authority prevailed—indeed, its sense became more widespread among masses of people because of its symbolic meaning. The British oath of military loyalty: "For King and Country" (note the absence of "The People") reflected this.*

But, either gradually or through revolutions, the interdependence—nay, the unity—of State and King was changing to that of State and People. And our concern here is with the decline of the authority and the power not of kings but of states. The principle of the near-absolute sovereignty of states had arisen—not always together, but often simultaneous with the sovereign authority of their different monarchs. A most important milestone was the 1648 Treaty of Westphalia, at the end of the Thirty Years' War. It was then that the principle and the practice of the sovereignty of states (this coincided with the then–ever more precise geographic definitions of their territories and frontiers) became

---

*In a very different state and country, in the Austro-Hungarian monarchy, the authority of the monarch and of the army—at least this was Franz Joseph's conviction—had to hold that ramshackle and multinational state together.

nearly universal in Europe. It had become part and parcel of international civilization. (This was when The European Age finally replaced the previous, largely Mediterranean one.) The then-great power and influence of European states, especially western and northern European ones, including Britain, the rapid expansion of their domains and colonies across the globe occurred together with the establishment of a European state system, a continuous web of their international relations, the extension of a previous small but significant state system in the Italies to almost all of Europe—lasting, in many ways, into the twentieth century. There were many consequences of this, including the practice of the European balance of power.

But there an important correction of terms is necessary. The then-new practice of international diplomacy, of permanent and regulated relations of states with most, if not all, other states was not really "international" but interstate. It involved, for a long time, states but not yet nations. The essence of this was that the sovereignty of states became even more important than the sovereignty of kings. Even in the instances of the most autocratic of monarchs the supreme importance of the state existed. The monarch ruled and represented the state, but he served the latter and not the reverse, not unlike the relationship of a father to his family. One example of this I found in the reminiscences of Countess Marion Doenhoff, writing about the Prussian aristocrats who attempted to kill Hitler in 1944. One of her ancestors,

Count Heinrich Yorck, "reminded his children from early youth on, that they must protect and defend the principles of the state, even against an occupant of the throne, if must."

But then, at the end of the eighteenth century and proceeding throughout the nineteenth, another element arose, marking the gradual decline of the aristocratic and the rise of the democratic age. Here and there (expressed definitely in the Constitution of the United States) the sovereignty of the people (or at least the image and the principle of the people) either replaced or diminished the authority of monarchs.* And this, naturally rather than unnaturally, led to a mutation of the purposes of the state, beyond the defense of the realm. The state would be more than the main instrument of the defense of the country; it would become *the* main instrument of the welfare of its people. Hence the origins and the ever more necessary laws and institutions of the welfare state. Consequently, the governmental powers of the state spread wider and wider. This demophile development inevitably involved the burgeoning of an ever-larger state bureaucracy. Whether this increase in the functions of government was unquestionably good or bad ought not be a matter for further speculation here. What belongs here is the recognition that in the twentieth century all of

*This could be easily misread: as we have seen in 1917–1918 when Wilson and American progressives hailed the victory over Germany as the world-historical victory of democracy over monarchical autocracy.

this happened together with something unexpected: with the general decline of the very authority of the state.

⁂

In the second half of the twentieth century, near the end of the Modern Age, the authority of and respect for the state, of this creation of the Modern Age, have been declining. Many things have contributed to this. They include the obvious limitations of the territorial sovereignty of states in an age of air (and, later, of space) travel; the increase of international commerce and trade; the increasing movement of goods and of people; the existence of international (more precisely: interstate and superstate) institutions, here and there over and above the sovereign authority of states. At another level: the, often evident, dissatisfaction of masses of people with the cumbrous, and sometimes stultifying, bureaucratic nature and uniformitarian institutions of modern states. And then, on another level: the exciting importance of nations when compared to that of states.

"Totalitarianism," and the—seemingly—all-pervasive power of police states have obscured the condition that almost everywhere state power has been weakening. After the collapse of Communism in Russia the critical problem has not been the undue power but the fatal weakness of the authority of the state. (President Putin has seen this, which is why he deserves at least some credit.) But the same development is there across Europe and most of the world. Those who in Britain—quite understandably—oppose joining "Europe" are worried about a fatal weakening of British self-government and of its traditions. And of course the "European Community" or "European Union" is neither a community nor a union. It is a huge and creaking bureaucratic machine, bereft of the authority of a government or of an army and of a state. Of course: a "Europe" of nations or indeed "a European nation" do not exist. The very banner of "Europe" is uninspiring, an ever-changing garland of circular stars, in a pale blue field, another imitation of the flags of NATO or indeed of the stars on the flag of the United States.

There is another particular difficulty, involving the United States. This is the confusion (more than the expectable overlapping) of three American ideas: State, Nation, People. The origins of this difficulty are latent in the Constitution. Who represents—even better, incarnates—the sovereignty of this country? "We the People," yes (though we have seen that this phrase was a late and rapid addition to the text in 1787). But then the authority of American government, no matter whence it derives, has to be that of a state. This state has to be a federal and central one, notwithstanding the original—and, through two hundred years, ever weakening—authority of its component states. And the Constitution collapsed in 1861, unable as it was to prevent the breakup of the country and the Civil War. That, not slavery, was what brought the Civil War about: Lincoln's decision to preserve the authority of the American Union.

There is another, protracted, difficulty: the nature of the American nation. Unlike other nation-states, the United States was never such. The characteristics of American nationality developed slowly (note that Tocqueville in *Democracy in America* wrote about "Anglo-Americans" throughout), and then altered considerably. The ethnic and demographic components of the population of the United States were ever-changing. And what "Americanism" amounted and still amounts to is something like a creed, the essence of which creed is an American nationalism. An American is (and he may be a recent immigrant) whoever accepts this creed publicly and convincingly, so much so that there must be no difference from that in his private beliefs.

Here enters another example of American split-mindedness (meaning the coexistence of essentially contradictory beliefs in the same mind). This is the frequent and recurring popular idea and slogan to the effect that Americanism means an opposition to Big Government, that the enemy of American freedom may be Washington, etc.—a belief especially propagated by American "conservatives," even though it is wholly contradictory. For the same people who oppose governmental regulations, bureaucracy, further and further applications and extensions of the American welfare state, are, more than often, believers in and vocal supporters of "defense" expenditures, of the army and navy and air and space programs, of more police powers, etc.—as if these were not "government." ("Liberals" often have the opposite priorities.) The now-traditional two-party system only confuses this further. A symbolic and symptomatic example of the confusion of state and nation and people is the cult of the American flag—a cult more sacrosanct than in many other countries. National flags, in Europe and elsewhere, emerged relatively late; in many states and countries they did not exist until the late eighteenth century, in many others not until a century later. There is a duality, a dual attraction of flags; the elements of this duality vary from country to country. They represent a particular state; but, more than that, they are also national symbols.* At the time of writing the current president of the United States chooses to wear an enamel badge of the Stars and Stripes constantly, on the lapel of every one of his suits and other garments— demonstrating that he is an American nationalist, that he belongs to the unexceptionable population of the United States.

In most places of the world the consciousness of na- tionality often preceded the existence and the institution of a state;[†] but often the existence and the institution of a state preceded and further crystallized the sense of nationality. What we must consider is that nations, and the conscious-

---

*Walter Bagehot, circa 1867: "The fancy of the mass of men is in- credibly weak; it can see nothing without a visible symbol, and there is much that it can scarcely make out without a symbol."

[†]About this Hitler was both right and wrong. "First came the *Volk;* only then came the *Reich.*" (Whence his argument, that the principle of the Third Reich was that of a Volkstaat, a folkish empire.) Yes: but not in the very national consciousness of the people.

ness of the nationality of people, may survive and even supersede the authority of the state.

Notwithstanding particular American conditions, in the United States, too, the weakening of the authority of the state proceeds. Legislation, and popular acceptance of privatization, deregulation, etc., are evidences of this. Yet this distrust of a federal government is not uniform: we have seen that those who—thoughtlessly—proclaim that "big government is the enemy" support, and enthusiastically, huge military and police and "space" expenditures. Meanwhile, the importance of giant corporations, involving their "globalization," is deceiving, because their transitory managers and directors are not their real owners. They do not amount to a new aristocracy, to the kind of aristocracy that inevitably arises when states are weakening. A new barbarian feudalism is bound to come in the future: but not yet.

In sum, we must not take comfort in the weakening of the state, which was a prime instrument of modern civilization. Cast a look at the recent history of South America. The triumph of Perón in October 1945 signified the protracted attraction of nationalist and populist socialism only a few months after Hitler and Mussolini had died. I glance at a photo of the broadly smiling Juan Domingo Perón and of his wife, Evita, with the nakedness of their fleshy faces, as they wave to an enormous crowd from the balcony of their palace in Buenos Aires. It is a picture of awesome vulgarity. It is less frightening than those images of Hitler in *Triumph* *of the Will* but *vulgar* to the utmost. And this in a country, in a part of the world, where people had, or still have, few or almost no commitments to the institutions of their states, while their minds are filled with a cheap heady froth of nationalism. Recently Mario Vargas Llosa put it in this way: "In Latin America there is a total lack of confidence on the part of the immense majority of the people, in institutions, and that is one of the reasons our institutions fail." (One of the reasons; but reason enough.*) "Institutions cannot flourish in a country if the people don't believe in them—if, on the contrary, people have a fundamental distrust of their institutions and see in them not a guarantee of security, or of justice, but precisely the opposite." Well, not perhaps "precisely" but largely so: among people whose populist nationalism (again: distinct from old-fashioned patriotism) is the only viscous bond—at the expense (and sometimes in defiance) of civilization—with its inevitable components of hatred and fear. Chesterton's great maxim is apposite here. "It is hatred that unites people—while love is always individual."

---

*Of course this varies from country to country—Chile being perhaps a significant exception.

{THE DECLINING FUNCTION OF "CLASSES"}

THE PASSAGE FROM aristocratic societies through their coexistence with the rise of democracy and the consequent universal acceptance and prevalence of popular sovereignty involves many matters other than politics. A decline of authority is evident in many fields of life. It is inseparable not only from what has happened in the relationships of states but from what has happened within nations and their classes.

In the past the shape of societies, the distribution of wealth and of authority within them, resembled something of a pyramid. More accurately: not quite a pyramid but rather a leaf with a small stem, or something like the ace of spades—because the very poorest were never the most numerous: the most numerous, the broadest stratum of a society, almost always comprised those of the lower working class, a tad above the poorest and the most destitute. That the growth of democracy was roughly parallel with the growth of the middle classes is obvious. But about one hundred years ago the middle classes were no longer merely in the middle between aristocrats and plebeians; both their numbers and their influence increased to an extent that the entire shape of societies, of the distribution of wealth and power within them, changed. By about 1900 certain countries such as (this list is neither complete nor accurate) the United States, most of the English-speaking ones, the Scandinavian nations had become overwhelmingly middle-class societies.* Latest by the 1920s in the United States the shape of social distribution no longer resembled a pyramid. It was, rather, the shape of an onion: rounder and rounder, with only a tiny upper and a small lower protuberance. It was not only that in the United States in 1927 almost two-thirds of families owned automobiles; more significantly, more than 80 percent of Americans identified themselves as "middle class"—a figure that, notwithstanding the fast development of The Onion, did not really correspond to actual figures of relative wealth or of income or of occupation. No matter: that was how people designated, or wished to designate, themselves. Another two or three generations later in America not only "middle class" but also "working class" were no longer accurate categories, nor even clearly or even approximately distinguishable.

The consequence of this has not been an entirely classless society, since there never was, is, or will be such a thing; but a society where "class" has largely lost its traditional meaning and function. This transformation had a profound

*This book is not a sociological treatise. Thus the very important and often lamentably obscured distinction between "middle class" and "bourgeois," as well as the subtle but very significant divisions between upper and lower middle classes, especially their cultural and civilizational differences, cannot belong here.

effect on social aspirations. Life is moved by the wish for more life; men and women are moved not only by their motives but by their purposes; they are drawn forward; the pull of the future is as important as the push of their past. The history of a society, or even of a nation, is largely formed by the aspirations of certain people. That the rise of political democracy from the seventeenth to the twentieth century was largely the result of social as well as political aspirations is obvious. What is less obvious is the state of aspirations in the largely (though not entirely) classless society in which we now live. Hence the following discussion, ostensibly but not entirely, about snobbery.

In a recent book, *Snobbery: The American Version,* the excellent essayist (a disappearing breed) Joseph Epstein wrote, "Snobbery as we know it today, snobbery meant to shore up one's own sense of importance, and to make others sorely feel their insignificance. . . . *It took the spread of democracy to make that possible*" (my italics). This is not so. Vanity; and class-consciousness; and the ingrained ideas and practices of status and of its privileges—the human pecking order— have always existed. (If not since Adam and Eve, then surely since Cain and Abel, not to speak of Abraham and Lot, etc.) But snobbery—at least in the sense we know it, or ought to know it—no. In an aristocratic and feudal world it was useless for a vassal (or even for a burgher) to pretend that he was one of the noble class, and hope to be included in the latter. Even in the fretful jostling of the men and women in Saint-Simon's Versailles the predominant impulses were those of vanity, not of snobbery: aiming at prestige and status rather than at social acceptance.

Snobbery, European and English snobbery, was a particular phenomenon not of the democratic age but of the past four or five centuries, marked by the increasing confluence and coexistence of Aristocracy and Democracy, when the former was declining and the latter rising. During its last phase, mostly during the nineteenth century, the political power of aristocracies was beginning to dissolve, while their social prestige continued to exist and attract. That was the best environment—the richest soil, the richest moisture, the richest atmosphere—for snobbery to flower.

In Europe and England, that was. The history of the word "snob" illustrates this. The legend is that "snob" was derived from old, usually eighteenth-century directories printing names, addresses, and titles, where "s.nob." was an abbreviation of "sine nobilitate": *not* a nobleman. Hence its pejorative meaning: a commoner who pretends not to be one, as in Molière's *Le Bourgeois Gentilhomme.* The *Oxford English Dictionary* lists various and obscure origins of the word, including one meaning a shoemaker's apprentice, and a mid-nineteenth-century one: "vulgar." Yet not every snob is a vulgarian, while vulgar men and women do not customarily aspire to be snobs. "Aspire" is the operative verb. The essence of snobbery consists of social aspirations, a powerful attraction that can be even stronger than attractions of sex or even of wealth. Hence the most poignant and telling aphorisms about snobs. "Were it not for imagination," Samuel Johnson said, "a man would be as happy in the arms of a chambermaid as of a duchess. But such is the adventitious charm of fancy, that we find men who have violated the best principles of society, and ruined their fame and fortune that they might possess a woman of rank." Stendhal, too, wrote that "a duchess is never more than thirty years old to a snob." Johnson and Stendhal were better observers than Virginia Woolf (herself a snob of a peculiar kind), who said that "the essence of snobbery is that you wish to impress other people." That is vanity, not snobbery, for the question is: what kind of people? The snob is both more and less than a social climber. By and large he is a social climber who cannot take his eyes off the upward rungs of the ladder, rather than a social climber who constantly and nervously keeps looking down at what and whom he left behind—someone who at best (or worst) takes good care to forget where he has sprung from so that there will be no recoil.

While snobs have been, on occasion, translated from Europe to America, European snobbery is untranslatable to the New World. The United States was never a classless society: but both the meaning and the structure of "class" in America was never, and is not now, like that in Europe or in England. Social mobility has been faster and more widespread in America than elsewhere; and it is social mobility that makes the snob—unless there is too much of it. When social mobility is rapid and widespread, this deprives him of many of his aspirations. (Whence the classic Groucho Marxism: not wanting to join a club which would have him as a member.) However—there was a period of American history when snobbery, though not dreadfully rampant, was both pervasive and fairly frequent. This was the period stretching from the Civil War for about a century, when class consciousness in America became strong (and especially among the newly rich and their descendants). From about 1870 to 1960 there existed barriers categorically excluding certain people—because of their provenance—from certain clubs, schools, institutions. At one end of society the remnant old patricians of eastern America retreated, while the fast-increasing mass of a middle class, including immigrants and their offspring, aimed not only at being accepted by their visible uppers and betters but at equaling them, by possessions and money. Most Americans, then as now, thought that the richest were the uppermost class, and that was that—yet it was not quite that simple, and the newly arrived rich knew it, too.

When class consciousness in America was strong, much of American literature was suffused with it. Some writers, like Henry James, were snobs themselves: they fled to the Old World to escape what they said was the absence of tradition and art in America, while it is at least arguable that what vexed James as much, if not more, was the absence of a genuine American upper class. Still, I must put in at least a good word for social aspirations. They produced not only lasting collections but lasting works of art, here in America. Their presence, invisible but audible, is there in the fine and sophisticated harmonies of American music composed by Gershwin, Arlen, Kern, etc., offspring of recent lower-class immigrants. *The Great Gatsby*, the finest of American romantic novels, portrayed a romantic desire, in which money is merely an instrument of aspiration to class.

But even when class consciousness in the New World was at its peak, snobbery in America was different from the Old World's. A decisive element in this difference was publicity. The older American patrician families resented and feared publicity. The newly arrived American Upper, or Richer, people wanted and desired it. Ward McAllister's list of the Four Hundred in New York, or the Social Register (both appearing first in the 1890s), as well as the social pages of American newspapers, large or small, were instruments of publicity. Social publicity, instead of firming up a class structure, resulted in the end and in a devolution, from Society (perhaps through the intermediate phase of "Café Society") to Celebrity. It is not a coincidence that society pages began to disappear from American newspapers around 1960, at the same time when the American noun "socialite" vanished, too, having had a definable one hundred–year run, from about 1860. In Mencken's *American Language*, Supplement One, "socialite" is listed, while "snob," curiously perhaps, does not appear at all. It may be telling that "dandy" and "dandyism" (closely related to snobbery) were never American phenomena: "dandy" and "toff" (the latter a more vulgar version of the former) never really took root in the United States. It may also be telling that the careers of such self-styled American social arbiters as Lucius Beebe or Cleveland Amory were unimaginable except for their publicity in newspapers and magazines.

A sociology professor (Judith N. Sklar) wrote that snobbery is "a repudiation of every democratic value." Not quite. Joseph Epstein wrote that "in the United States contempt for social inferiors more than anything else marked the snob." If so, then the prototypes of snobs are mere kids— teenagers who are ready to snub and hurt those classmates who wear cheaper sneakers. But the true snob's admiration for superior people is almost always stronger than is his contempt for social inferiors. Nor does the snob care much for material possessions, except perhaps for his clothes. When the men and women the snob admires are unimpressed with the houses and cars and furnishings and pieces of art and vacation places and club memberships that other people possess, the snob won't be impressed either. The best one can say for a genuine snob is that he values taste rather than judgment—indeed, often at the expense of his own judgment. That is not always wrong.

"Anti-Semitism may itself be the first and perhaps the longest lasting and most virulent form of snobbery." No: prejudice and snobbery are not the same things. At his worst, a snob prejudges; at his best, he discriminates. And in an increasingly classless society discrimination remains a matter for individuals, not for groups. An ever-changing variety of groups will continue to exist, even in a classless society: Political (liberal or conservative) snobs who constitute not social classes but classes of opinion, Wine Snobs, Food Snobs, Travel Snobs, etc., etc., however ephemeral. Status, money, possessions: their differences will always exist, even in America. Now that Society has been just about entirely replaced by Celebrity (which, by its very nature, is ephemeral), the relatively recent usage of "it has class," "classy," "a class act" are merely stumbling phrases in search of some kind of definition within what has now become an increasingly fluid population. "World-class," for example, is just about devoid of meaning—like "upscale," which means only something that is a tad more expensive than are other similar things.

Men and women wishing to associate—indeed, to be associated—with the rich and famous (note the increasing confluence of these two categories) will go on and on, forever. But there is something about snobs and snobbery that seems ever more old-fashioned. It is even possible that "snob" (like "s.nob.") may sooner or later be classed in dictionaries as *obs.:* obsolete. One interesting feature of both American class consciousness and snobbery is the relatively recent positive connotation of the adjective "old-fashioned," together with the rapid decline of the reputation of "modern." It may even lead to the appearance of a new kind of snobbishness whose essence will be a respect not for anything fashionably avant-garde but for history. (Could be worse. . . .)

The decline of democracy toward populism may not be inevitable; but it has been inseparable from the decline of authority. ("Authority" derives from "autoritas," that is: authorship, moral, social or legal position, dependent on the ability to speak clearly.) The disappearance of the subtle authority of an upper class is but one example of that. It also involves the decline of authority within families. There are multiple evidences of this, ranging from the cult of youth through the increase of criminality among the young to the puerilism of so many adults. A desire for authority will not vanish among men and women; but it may take unexpected and perhaps even shocking new forms.

One example of the crisis of authority now involves the Roman Catholic Church—which may be, after all, the last hierarchical institution in the world. To reconcile the church with democracy has not been easy, but it has not been insuperable. During the past two hundred years there were particular glitches and hiccups in the relationship of Catholic authority and American democracy; but they eventually went away, for many reasons, including the accord of American Catholics with American nationalism. (The total separation of church and state in America was seldom anything but a constitutional illusion; asserted on occasion and then disappearing fast, the essence of the matter being the rarity of any enduring conflict between the American church and popular sovereignty.)

{ "TYRANNY OF THE MAJORITY"? "PUBLIC
OPINION" AND ITS MISREADINGS }

A S THE FORMER LIBERAL MEANING of democracy devolves toward populism, the danger of tyranny by the majority arises. The phrasing of this was Tocqueville's great contribution to the "science" of politics about one hundred and seventy years ago. Almost exactly a century later Ortega y Gasset, in *The Revolt of the Masses*, invented the phrase of "modern Mass Man." Tocqueville saw, first in America, the often deadening, rather than invigorating, power of mass public opinion, a somewhat new kind of danger different from the dangers of untrammeled democracy that Aristotle and others had asserted. A majority is not inherently right for having been a properly elected majority; a majority, like an aristocratic minority, or like a monarch, may be right or wrong; and when it is wrong, to change it or its consequences may be long, arduous, for a while seeming hopeless. Ortega y Gasset wrote less about majorities than about sheer numbers, about the masses made up by men whose opinions and ideas, whose physical and, more important, mental behavior may be unoriginal, middling, crude. Tocqueville and Ortega y Gasset were not the only thinkers and writers who were pessimistic about the behavior of masses. In any event, their diagnoses and analyses were more telling and more profound than those of "progressives" and leftists who—not only superficially but insincerely*—idealized The Common Man.

But now we must go further. Tocqueville and Ortega y Gasset (and they were rather different men) wrote about the pathogenesis of public opinions. But the functions of opinions, their propagations and the effects and the extensions and the protraction and the endurance of opinions in the democratic age, are not what they were in the past. No matter how powerful or even practical an idea, or advocacy, or opinion, its effect is almost wholly dependent on its distribution, on its acceptance. It is sometimes possible to trace the origin of, say, a royal decision or policy, stimulated by an adviser; of course the monarch must have been, at least potentially, receptive to the idea; and then this potentiality coagulated into actuality at a sometimes ascertainable and recognizable moment. But when it comes to a modern democratic political idea or advertising slogan—whatever its

*Insincerely: because most of them regarded themselves as the natural intellectual or political leaders in a new "classless" society of plain people.

validity—its public appearance, meaning its actual acceptance by the managers of a president of a party or of a firm,
is calculated (if that is the proper verb) *together* with its potentiality *at the same instant.*

Certain questions—or, rather, distinctions—arise here.
Does democracy mean the reign of public opinion? No,
rather than yes: because "public opinion," as such, belonged
rather to the nineteenth century; it was the opinion, and
often the accepted opinion, of the middle classes. (Bagehot:
the opinion "of the bald gentlemen sitting in the back of the
omnibus.") Moreover, in that now more and more remote
past, there were still appreciable differences between opinions and sentiments. "Public opinion"—its assertion, its
research, its measurement, the polls in our times, indeed
throughout the twentieth century—has been all too often
confused with popular sentiment. But "public" and "popular," "opinion" and "sentiment" are not the same things.
Throughout the twentieth century, and even during dictatorships, there are many examples of public opinions having had accumulating effects on private opinions and also
on popular sentiments, involving even the very words people
were going to use. (Hitler knew this very well, whence his
conviction that certain ideas and slogans must be repeated
and repeated in order to assure their popular support.) On the
other hand, popular sentiments—once they are sufficiently
widespread to allow their frequent public appearances—
may coagulate into the decisive weakening, indeed, gradual

disappearance, of previously accepted public ideas and slogans (as, for example, in the case of the disestablishment of
most Communist regimes in Eastern Europe in the 1980s).
But in the Western democracies, too, the differences between publicly stated opinions and private or even popular
sentiments are often recognizable (though seldom so re-
corded by historians who ought to know better).*

The problem—and it is a historical problem—exists
therefore not only with the origins of ideas but with what is
often imprecisely called public opinion.† What historians
sometimes can, and should, ascertain is perhaps not so
much the origin of ideas but how ideas move. Here Tocqueville is again pertinent. He believed, and wrote, that ideas,
indeed intellectual life, in the democratic age move, and will
move, very slowly. His contemporaries—conservatives as
well as radicals, pessimistic aristocrats as well as optimistic
liberals—believed that with the rise of democracy ideas
would gather speed, sometimes dangerously so: that the

---

*One example. Unanimous or near-unanimous congressional votes
such as the often 435:0 in favor of American support to Israel do not accurately prove, or even indicate, that the private or even the popular sentiments of Americans in that regard are universal or even uniform.

†Someone once wrote that the road to the truth goes through a
graveyard of untruths. This is so—except that those graveyards have become jungles, not only marked by broken and abandoned stones but full
of rampant weeds, the rampant weeds being accepted ideas and opinions. Flaubert recognized this in his unfinished masterpiece, *Bouvard et
Pécuchet.*

awakened populations would force the political and social
to swing to extremes, perhaps from one extreme to the other.
Tocqueville, in America, recognized the very opposite. He
wrote not only that the monstrous accumulating weight of
public opinion might lead to (or even constitute) a tyranny
of the majority, but that it actually slows down the movement of ideas, dependent as those are on their acceptability
by large masses of people. He foresaw the considerable and
often dangerous condition of democratic stagnation, in intellectual as well as in political life. A good example of this
is what I may call the momentum of opinions, a kind of
protracted and long-enduring deadweight. Here are three
examples. American reaction against American intervention in the First World War in 1917—and against the then-
extreme anti-German ideas—gathered slowly, appearing
here and there in the early 1920s, and then gathering momentum, reaching its very peaks around 1936–1937, when a
new German danger, with Hitler, was already occurring.
This popular reaction (sometimes imprecisely equated with
"isolationism") was a difficult problem for Franklin Roosevelt; he chose to deal with it subtly and slowly. Or: the
peak of the popularity of anti-Communism was at its highest in the United States in the 1950s (and enduring there
even in the Reagan era of the 1980s), when both Communism and the Soviet Union were already in retreat. (In the
1930s that condition of public opinion was a handicap for
Roosevelt and for an intelligent conduct of American for-

eign policy; in the 1980s it was not, since the managers of foreign policy and of intelligence thought it best to be in accord with it, indeed, to profit from it.) A third example, proof of the often deadening slowness of minds not among the so-called masses but among intellectuals: the recognition of many French intellectuals of the evils of Communism as late as 1956 and after, and then the intellectual and popular fashionableness of anti-Communism in France as late as the 1970s. So much for the proverbial quickness of French minds. . . .

DECLINE OF PRIVACY, RISE OF PUBLICITY

PRIVACY WAS NOT CUSTOMARY—indeed, it was hardly a virtue—during the Middle Ages. It began to be appreciated after 1600 (coterminous with the first appearance in English of the word "civilization"). It had much to do with the then-rising ideal of "home." Gradually, here and there, the idea of privacy acquired legal protection; it became part and parcel of political constitutions. Three hundred years later, at the end of the Modern Age, the emphasis on privacy, and on its—often bourgeois—customs and habits, has been eroding.

Contradictory—indeed, schizophrenic—tendencies have been at work. On the one hand—in what may be one of the last, feeble insistences of a decaying liberalism—states and governments are being badgered to extend more and more "liberties" to individuals, amounting to their "rights." On the other hand, the instruments of supermodern technology and "communications" (not to speak of all kinds of instruments of surveillance) cut deep inroads into private lives and private communications. But even more important is the amplitude of evidence to the effect that the desire for privacy among people has begun to erode. There are myriad examples of this. It may be sufficient to notice that the—never complete, but for a long time respected, and in some instances even sacrosanct—distinction between private and public convictions, ideas, appearances, customs has become badly confused. "Esse quam videri"—to be more than to seem—is a mark of maturity, the opposite of puerilism. The main purpose of the latter is "to seem," to get public approval; "being" has become a rarity, just as men and women with considerably independent minds are now rarae aves. Since our subject is—largely—that of politics and of power, we may as well essay the question whether Machiavelli has not become outdated too? His, once radically realistic, startling recognition of the sometimes inevitable need for hypocrisy as a result of the sometimes necessary difference between private thoughts and public expressions, could exist only in a world where vice was forced to pay tribute to virtue, and not in a world where whatever is or be-

comes public overwhelms whatever remains of private convictions—among other things, overwhelming not a few of
the once distinctions between virtue and vice.

Our theme now is not that of Mass Man or the Tyranny
of the Majority: obvious dangers due to the thoughtless acceptance of the supreme power of popularity. It is something else (though related to the former): the cult and culture of publicity. That liberal democracy may devolve to a
cult (or at least government) by popularity was foreseeable,
more or less. That the United States, founded as a republic,
turned into a popular democracy by the time of Andrew
Jackson's election in 1828 (every one of the previous presidents had belonged, or were intimately connected, to the
Founding Fathers) is commonplace historical knowledge.
Tocqueville understood that well; after all, he visited America during Jackson's presidency.* Yet his insights into the
functioning of democracy went much wider (and deeper)
than to the sphere of politics. His paragraphs about public
opinion and about the pressures of democratic conformity
suggested something that he elucidated in another chapter
("Some Characteristics of Historians in the Democratic
Age"), in one or two brilliantly concise paragraphs: that the
history of democratic peoples may be something easy to
write superficially but not really adequately, because popu-

*One important condition that existed then but weakened there-
after: the president's authority was not yet overwhelming. The imperial
presidency was something that the great prophet of the democratic age
did not foresee.

larity is a complicated phenomenon, because of its propagation, because of its functions. By repeating and repeating
that someone or something is popular we may indeed make
him or it popular—at least for a time.

"Populist" was not yet a political term or designation in
Tocqueville's time (it appeared one or two generations after
his death). But the measuring of popularity had already
begun. With the extension of suffrage, elections were only
one measure of relative popularities. Gradually the very selection of electoral candidates came to depend more and
more on their selectors' assessment of a nominee's potential
popularity, often overriding some of the selectors' concerns
about the nominee's merits. Gradually, too, not only did
the mass of voters grow but the very procedures of the selection and nomination of candidates became more and
more democratic (as, for example, in the Seventeenth
Amendment to the Constitution, providing for the popular
selection of senatorial candidates through "primaries"—
another "progressive" improvement with questionable results). The increasingly frequent taking of the pulse of potential electoral preferences (inaccurately termed as "public
opinion" polls) came gradually, too—eventually to an extent where the results of elections could be projected, re-
ported, and indeed furthered well in advance. Eventually
matters degenerated to an extent where pollsters were hired
by contending parties, for the purpose of announcing "results" of "public opinion" (more precisely: of electoral preferences), numbers that could be, and often were, skewed,

inflated, manufactured for the purpose of affirming the popularity of a candidate by asserting his popularity.

While in Europe there were states where the percentage of voters was high (and some even where voting was practically obligatory), in the United States the proportion of actual voters began to fall—interestingly enough, in 1920 and after, when an amendment had given women the vote. Again, those who encouraged more and more people to vote (one dubious result of this being the Twenty-Sixth Amendment, granting the right to vote to eighteen-year-old youth), among other things making voting and registration to vote ever easier, were wrong rather than right. In so many instances demagogic or otherwise corrupt candidates have been elected when suddenly more rather than fewer people were voting. There may be room for an argument that, for the sake of proper democracy, voting should be made not easier but more difficult, whereby the electoral majority would be the result of a more, not less, responsible citizenry— just as the time has already come for restricting, instead of increasing, automobile traffic for the sake of easing travel.

In any event—the sanctimoniousness of the election process may blind people to the obvious dangers of further technical "progress." During the near-constitutional crisis in November–December 2000, during the fiddling and counting of contested votes in Florida, not one of the many thousands of articles and editorials and letters to editors spoke in favor of returning to paper ballots. The myth of technology ruled supreme. There was nearly universal support for Congress to mandate uniform technical instruments of voting machines in every American hamlet—this when any teenage hacker can juggle or fix computers and their results. No one questioned how the counting of votes may (yes, they can) be manipulated through computers, with considerable ease, with results very difficult to detect. In the vast country of Canada paper ballots were still used in 2000, and the national election results were counted within a few hours. In Brazil voters were told to sit in front of computers and poke their fingers at colored squares on the screen. An editorial in the *New York Times* proposed that Congress consider adopting the Brazilian practice.*

{PUBLICITY AND CELEBRITY}

B UT THERE CAME A NEW DEVELOPMENT, something that even a Tocqueville or a Burckhardt did not and perhaps even could not consider. This was the rising and eventually overwhelming influence of publicity, of its manipulations and of its ever more pervasive presence. This was not a simple matter—indeed, often a new kind of dan-

*In my diary I wrote: "We are on the way of becoming not yet a banana republic but a banana democracy."

ger to democracy, less direct but perhaps even more insidious than that of the tyranny of a majority, since it is more than often the decisive influence of certain insistent and powerful minorities. James Fenimore Cooper (Tocqueville's near-contemporary) recognized this early, in 1838, in *The American Democrat*. The efforts "to create publick opinion," he wrote, "is to *simulate* the existence of a general feeling in favor, or against, any particular man, or measure; so great being the deference paid to publick opinion, in a country like this, that men actually yield their own sentiments to that which they believe to be the sentiment of the majority." So this sensitive early American writer was worried less by the prospect of a tyranny of the majority or even with the deference paid to public opinion than with its simulation: something different from direct populism.

In 1791, according to *The Oxford English Dictionary*, "publicity" meant "The quality of being public; the condition or fact of being open to public observation or knowledge." But by 1904 it had become "the business of making goods or persons publicly known." Less than twenty years later "publicity agent," "public relations," "public relations expert," "the public relations industry" or "business" (all of them Americanisms)* became current. Some of these terms and their profitable employment were due to Edward L. Bernays circa 1920 (incidentally a relative of Sigmund Freud).

---

*But of course this was not an American *novum*. The first American Public Relations Figure (indeed, Expert) was Benjamin Franklin.

A generation later the term "P.R." had become part of the American vocabulary—and soon part of many other languages. Ever since then the functioning and the "measuring" of "public opinion" and of its simulation, or manufacture, began to overlap—as in more than one instance the purposes of public relations agents and of pollsters: the generating of publicness, even more than that of "opinion." Thus the second transformation of the American political system, from popularity contests to publicity contests, had begun.*

This involved, among other things, a condition for which majority rule or its potential tyranny were no longer a sufficient explanation. There has come the ever recurring presence of "hard" minorities and "soft" majorities, with the former capable of influencing or even governing the latter. Such influences are not fixable or ascertainable by numbers; they are not the sheer results of quantities or of deadweight.

For some time now there have been but two elective (elective, and not hereditary) monarchs in the world: the president of the United States of America, and the pope of the Holy Roman Catholic and Apostolic Church. The great historian Johan Huizinga described how imagination and life in the Middle Ages were public and visual. The shift to

---

*A very telling example was the primary law enacted by the state of Oregon in 1954. According to it, "the names of those persons who the Secretary of the State of Oregon determines in his sole discretion to be 'generally advocated or recognized in national news media throughout the United States' as presidential candidates are placed on the ballot." That is: the nominators are "the national news media," rather than the people.

the pictorialization of American imagination (that had begun well before the ubiquity of television) as well as the great growth of bureaucratization affected the very functioning of the American presidency after 1920. Whereas in the case of hereditary monarchies the intrusion of publicity inevitably weakened and often damaged the authority of the monarch (as it would be the case with the father of a family), in more than one way the American elective monarchy contained elements of neo-medievalization. American presidents now depended on a court of advisers who planned his public appearances and who presented not only various options of policy but the very selection and the formulation of those "issues" which, in their opinion, and always with a narrow eye on immediate publicity, the elective monarch had to address (or, more precisely, convincingly seem to address). Dwight Eisenhower was the first television president. (In 1948 Harry Truman appeared on television only for three minutes, urging the citizenry to vote.) In 1952 Eisenhower's staff hired the actor Robert Montgomery to prepare Eisenhower's television grooming and appearances; Montgomery remained on the White House staff for some time. In 1956 another actor, George Murphy (who eventually became a senator from California, the beginning of an obvious trend there) took Montgomery's place. This transformation of the election campaigns and the transformation of the presidency from popularity to publicity contests of course involved enormous sums of money, especially because of television. (As always, such a vast expenditure of public monies and their inherent corruption was not so much cause as effect.) It was also inseparable from the incessant growth of a vast "executive" bureaucracy (never pointed out by those "conservatives" who kept haranguing against Big Government).* In the Middle Ages—indeed, until about the seventeenth century—kings had no specialized ministries; they depended on the councils of intimate advisers. In the second half of the twentieth century the elective monarchy of the American presidency assumed more and more of the characteristics of medieval kingship, with liege lords having the power to determine the very access to the monarch, to the extent that even cabinet officers could no longer call on the president on their own—that is, without the consent of the abovementioned liege lords, who decided not only what and whom the president should see but also what he should hear—and perhaps subsequently think.

This near-absolute preoccupation with publicity involved, at least indirectly, an underestimation of the intellectual qualities of a president; but it involved, too, an underestimation of that of the American people. One symptom of this mutation of the political process from a popularity contest to a publicity contest was that, latest by 1980, the very word "popular" was fading in political usage, whereas "image"

*One example: in the 1980s the staff of Ronald Reagan's *wife* in the White House was larger than Franklin Roosevelt's at the height of the Second World War.

and "publicity" became more and more frequent.* This devolution involved something lamentable and insiduous: the
cult of celebrity. Movie actors, actresses, athletes were no
longer only useful instruments to enhance the electoral
prospects of a president or a senator. In more and more instances (the ridiculous example of Schwarzenegger in California, 2003 is but one example of this) their very celebrity
made them potential and successful candidates for high
public offices. This development, or devolution, went of
course well beyond elections. It involved the transformation
of society. The older American patriciandom, perhaps especially in the older cities of eastern America, attempted to
avoid celebrity while preserving privacy; but, latest after
1950, "Society" had more and more to do with Celebrity.
After all, celebrity means to be publicly known: the bridge
between Society and Celebrity consists of publicity; and
publicity will have an inevitable effect on people whose
discriminating manners are not matched by discriminating mental interests of their own. Celebrity may of course
be, and often is, ephemeral: in Joseph Conrad's words,
"the shame of undeserved success." Or, as an English poet
wrote in the seventeenth century: "An habitation giddy and
unsure / Hath he that buildeth on the vulgar heart." More
than three hundred years later, in 2003, the English writer
Clive James observed, indeed convincingly, that "the general

*As late as 1958 a sign on a Nantucket beach (drafted by Yankee
selectmen?): "On Nantucket Island bikini-style suits are not popular."
Such a usage of "popular" vanished soon thereafter.

spread of education didn't make people more resistant to fame. If anything, it made them *less* resistant."*

In the life of a man the decline of his powers in old age more than often results in his reversion to infantile habits, to a weakening of physical, and sometimes mental, controls. There may be some things similar in the devolution of a people. Again the wisdom of Johan Huizinga, the worthy successor of Tocqueville and of Burckhardt, is telling. "Puerilism," he wrote in the 1920s, is "the attitude of a community whose behavior is more immature than the state of its intellectual and critical faculties would warrant, which instead of making the boy into the man adopts the conduct of that of the adolescent age." Lamentably enough this is not an imprecise description of recent American presidents—and then some. But then it was Jakob Burckhardt who, long before the modern cult of publicity and celebrity, wrote about the Italian aspirations to leadership at the time of the Renaissance—that is, at the very dawn of the Modern Age:

> The highly gifted man of that day thought to find it
> in the sentiment of honour. . . . This sense of hon-
> our is compatible with much selfishness and great
> vices, and may be the victim of astonishing illusions;
> yet, nevertheless, all the noble elements that are left

---

*Allow me to say that I, for one, sometimes see in the cult of Celebrity something satanic or at least near-satanic—i.e., worse than the tyranny of the majority, and something, at least potentially, reminiscent of the Anti-Christ, as in the warnings of St. John and the Apocalypse.

in the wreck of a character may gather around it, and from this fountain may draw new strength. . . . It is certainly not easy, in treating of the Italian of this period, to distinguish the sense of honour from the passion for fame, into which, indeed, it may easily pass. Yet the two sentiments are essentially different.

In our times (I wrote more than twenty years ago), toward the end of the Modern Age, the difference—indeed, the increased discrepancy—between fame and honor has become so large that in the characters of presidents and in those of most public figures in all kinds of occupation, the passion for fame has just about obliterated the now remote and ancient sense of honor.

{CHANGES IN THE RECORDING AND
KNOWLEDGE OF HISTORY}

WE HAVE NOW SEEN that the original (and still common) idea that democracy, that democratic politics and democratic societies, would be more open, more direct, more simple than the order and the societies of the past, did not come about. The democratic order (or disorder) of people and things has become ever more complicated.

Perhaps at the bottom of all of this is the condition that "simple" people are not truly simple; or, rather, that the simple people of the past, largely unschooled men and women close to the soil, are, by and large, disappearing in an increasingly bureaucratic and intellectualized world. (And also that puerile men and women are less simple than are mature people.) However—complex indeed is the condition of modern democracy, of the sovereignty and rule of "the people." For who are "the people"? Statements by the people are almost always made in the name of the people— that is, one step away from simplicity, directness, authenticity. Yes: statements made in the name of the people in many instances may correspond to what the people, or at least most of them, think, say, and want: but these correspondences, when they exist, are necessarily ephemeral. "People feel," "people think," "people want," "people desire" cannot be taken as something accurate, or even properly ascertainable. At the same time they may be effective and useful and not devoid of considerable reality or even truth.

One reason for this is that what happens is inseparable from what people think happens—at least for a while. But the reconstruction—the history—of this is another (and growing) problem. In "Some Characteristics of Historians in the Democratic Age" Tocqueville summed up the essence of their problem—contrasting, as was his wont, aristocratic and democratic ages and their habits—in a stunning summary of forty-eight sentences. He wrote that while in aristocratic ages the temptation of chroniclers may have been the necessary and perhaps often superficial exaggeration of the importance of certain outstanding personalities, in the coming democratic age the temptation of historians may be the exaggeration of the importance and of the influence of general ideas (of economic and social "causes"), overlooking the complexities of events and peoples and the existence of free will.

The problems of historians in democratic ages are many. At the bottom of their problems is that of the recognition and the reconstruction of authenticity. "The people demanded," "the people wanted," "the people resisted," etc., etc. But: who were the people? When someone says or writes: "Napoleon said," or "Bismarck wanted," or "Lincoln denied," the evidence for that may or may not be proved. But who were "the people"? What is the evidence? Yes, there is some; and no, there is none. The writer of their history may be right; but he may also be wrong. Electoral statistics may help—but only in a limited way, registering a necessarily imposed choice between two or among a few more. "Opinion polls" even less so: imprecise and evanescent partial ascertainments of majorities as they are, at best (or at worst). Other problems for historians of the democratic age and of democratic societies are too numerous to mention. Contrary to what had been expected, the openness of democratic archives has made the tasks of researchers more and not less difficult. What has happened is a fantastic proliferation of papers and of other records and documents of all kinds, together with their deteriorating quality and authenticity. The once-sacrosanct canon of the difference between primary and secondary documents makes less and less sense now when, for example, even personal letters by presidents are often not only not drafted but not even dictated or signed by them. There is yet another relatively new condition. So many communications remain unrecorded; and the records and secret papers of entire governmental agencies may never be accessible at all.

However: the problems go beyond and beneath the difficulties of professional historians. Beyond and beneath the problem of the eventual reconstruction of what people wanted we must recognize the constantly increasing influence of mind into matter in the very lives of people. This influence is, probably inevitably, inseparable from inflation, which, in turn, seems to be a fundamentally democratic phenomenon. Consider, if only for a moment, the virtual vanishing of the inflation-deflation "business cycles." What we, in reality, experience is a constant increase of inflation* (true, sometimes faster, sometimes slower, but still)—and, therefore, the dematerialization of money and of possessions, especially in societies where creditability has become more important than actual possessions (which may be legally "owned" but are, in reality, rented). This—often false— spiritualization of matter, this present and ever-increasing intrusion of mind into matter has led to a world where

---

*The inflation of words (and, perhaps, of pictures and images, too) led to the inflation of money and of possessions—and not the other way around.

more and more images and abstractions influence more and more people—abstractions and images that are presentations of prearranged "realities" rather than representations of them.

All of this renders what we may call the structure of events more and more complex. One (but only one) example of this exists within the development of international relations. The word "international," thus employed in the nineteenth and twentieth centuries, has been imprecise (and, at least potentially, misleading). International relations, international law, international institutions, international organizations (thus the monstrously misnamed United Nations in 1945) involved states and governments, not nations and peoples. But then, ever more due to the increase of communications and of travel (and, even more important, of literacy), contacts and images of other peoples began to appear within nations. In 1800 a German peasant, say, in the midst of Brandenburg, was unlikely ever to have seen an Englishman. By 1900 he saw many of them, either in the flesh (as tourists) or, much more often, from pictures or drawings and even articles in newspapers. A consequence of this for historians was the necessary broadening—and deepening—of what in the past used to be "diplomatic" to a more recent international history, a much more difficult and complex reconstruction that few have, as yet, succeeded to accomplish more or less perfectly.

The importance of this, and of many other related matters, goes beyond the problems and methods of professional historians—because all thinking, including imagination, involves and depends on reconstruction; because perception inevitably depends on memory; because all cognition involves, and depends on, recognition. "We live forward; but we can only think backward" (Kierkegaard).

Yet there is a relatively new phenomenon, one of the few positive symptoms at a time otherwise suffused with decadence and with more and more apparent barbarism. This is an appetite for history, which in recent decades has involved peoples and classes who had hitherto been not only ignorant of but indifferent to it. Of course appetite may be corrupt or corrupted, wrongly fed by junk food; still, the very existence of appetite is a sign of health. The evidences of this new and wide appetite for history are protean; this is not the place even to list them properly. They include, among other things, the surprising popularity of biographies (and the high qualities of some of them). Even more telling is the nearly complete reversal of the roles of history and novel, the ratio of their popularity as well as of the reversal of their perspectives. The novel (which, despite its few forerunners, was not a classic literary form) and professional historianship appeared at the same time, only little more than two hundred and fifty years ago. Each was the result of a newly developing historical consciousness, as well as the interest of the literate middle classes to read about men and women and places that were not idealized and legendary but recognizable to them: the description of lives and aspirations with which they could identify. However: by the middle of the twentieth century and thereafter all kinds of histories began to outsell novels. There occurred, too, a reversal of the relationship of history and "fiction." While in the past (and especially during the nineteenth century) novelists often used history as a colorful background for their stories (the historical novel), as the twentieth century moved ahead more and more novelists have been preoccupied or interested in history to an extent that in their—often imperfect and even illegitimate—confections history *is* the foreground, that is, the main topic. Most of such novelists do not really know what it is that they are doing. At the same time, many academic historians are blissfully unaware of this roiling, burgeoning appetite for history, and what this might mean for their craft.

A Polish poet, Adam Zagajewski, understood this. He recently wrote:

> I'm not a historian but I'd like literature to assume, *consciously and in all seriousness* [my italics], the function of a historical chronicle. I don't want it to follow the example set by modern historians, cold fish by and large, who spent their lives in vanquished archives and write in an inhuman, ugly, wooden, bureaucratic language from which all poetry's been driven, a language flat as a wood louse and petty as

the daily paper. I'd like it to return to earlier examples, maybe even Greek, to the ideal of the historian poet, a person who either has seen and experienced what he describes for himself, or has drawn upon a living oral tradition, his family's or his tribe's, who doesn't fear engagement and emotion, but who cares nonetheless about his story's thoughtfulness.

A NEW WORLD is now coming about, a new historic age, in which the predominance of America is a factor but only a factor, an instrument for a different confection of events. "A new science of politics" . . .—well, not really A Science, and perhaps not even "politics." However: human nature does not truly change. We have seen that, among other things, "conservative" and "liberal" have lost much, almost all, of their meanings. But "Right" and "Left," in their widest and deepest sense, still remain with us, especially at their extremes. And now let me state something that may be startling. One of the fundamental differences between extremes of Right and Left is this: in most instances hatred moves the former; fear the latter.

It was not always thus. Two hundred years ago the old "Right," authoritarian kingdoms and dukedoms, the conservatives and the aristocracies and their police, were fearful of the ideas of the French Revolution, of their attractions, and of their potential votaries. This is what, a generation before Victor Hugo or Dumas, Stendhal's *Charterhouse of Parma* is about, a book that circa 1945 some French and American intellectuals rediscovered as a literary paradigm, a microcosm of early "totalitarian" regimes—wrongly so. The Left (young 150 years ago, but no longer now) hated such regimes. That hatred bubbles through the writings of such otherwise different men as Marx or the Russian revolutionaries of the nineteenth century. They hate the rulers and the police, and when they fear them, that fear is mixed with contempt.

We have seen that some time after 1870 there came a change. Nationalism was replacing the older forms of patriotism, and it proved to be an even stronger and more lasting bond for masses of people than their consciousness about the struggle of classes. Its extreme representations and incarnations involved more than a dislike of foreigners. It included a contemptuous hatred of people within their own countries whom such nationalists saw as being insufficiently or even treasonably nonnationalist. This was no longer an aristocratic or even a conservative phenomenon but a populist one. It appeared in a great variety of nations and states; it attracted many revolutionary young; and their opponents soon learned to fear them.

We have seen that seventy years after Marx's *Communist Manifesto* the working classes in the capitalist states of the world were largely immune to Communism. In the history of the world the Communist revolution in Russia in 1917 was an anomaly. There were no successful Communist revolutions anywhere then, except for Russia, a country that Marx, at least for a long time, had excluded categorically from his projections of communism. All of this is well known. Less well known are the evidences of how afraid the Communist leaders were of nationalists. A few days before their coup in St. Petersburg (for that was what it was, not a real revolution) Lenin's cohorts thought it useful to address the Cossack regiments in St. Petersburg on posters, with the heading: "Cossacks! Brothers!"—this to the most hated and feared military symbols of the old regime. The Bolsheviks were right: the Cossacks in 1917 were not inclined to risk their skins to defend Kerensky and Co., those loquacious liberal townies in their frock coats.

Further evidences are protean. In the acts of the short-lived Communist attempts in Europe in 1919, in Munich or Budapest—including their most revolting terrorist acts—there is always the underlying, and often very apparent, element of fear: fear of their unpopularity, not only among the former ruling classes but among the masses. The same kind of fear was even more evident and persistent among the Communist rulers of the states of Eastern Europe after 1945, no matter how entrenched they were there by Stalin. And when it comes to international Communists, both before and after the last war, it does not take a psychologist to detect fear, even stronger than hatred, the fear of being a small minority, typical of most Communist intellectuals.

Of course fear, like all primal human phenomena, is not simple, and it is often allied, if not combined, with hatred. But it may be an acceptable generalization to state that, at least in the Western world, the ideas of Communist and of pro-Communist intellectuals in the twentieth century were inseparable from their fears: their fears of oppressive capitalists, their fear of "fascists," of "reactionaries," of the nationalist masses, of the conspiratorial powers of their opponents—compensated or, rather, clothed by their intellectual belief that their ideology was the only progressive one, marking the path to the future, their future.

This does not mean that all Communists were cowards. A sense of fear and an inclination to cowardice are not the same things. Courage is "grace under pressure," Hemingway wrote. Tell this to a soldier in a foxhole: bullshit about bullfighting, he would say. Courage is the ability to overcome one's fear, someone else said: and that is something that every combat soldier knows in the marrow of his bones.

For one thing, Stalin was not a coward. Yet it was his fear of his potential rather than actual opponents that explains the senseless and brutal extent of his purges in the 1930s. And when he and Molotov finally, and reluctantly, realized that Hitler was invading Russia, their immediate reactions were among the most abject ones in the history of statesmanship. Hitler had declared his war; his planes were bombing Russian towns; thousands of German tanks were driving into Russia in enormous clouds of dust; and Stalin's ambassador to Berlin, Dekanozov, one of his closest henchmen, babbled to Ribbentrop: "Are you sure there isn't a mistake?"—while Molotov said to the German ambassador in Moscow: "Did we deserve this?" But then the Russians defeated the Germans. Such is the irony of history—or, rather, of human nature.

No less a statesman than Winston Churchill recognized this. In 1950 he wrote: "The central factor of Soviet policy was fear. . . . Moscow feared our friendship more than our enmity. . . . The growing strength of the West would reverse this, so that they would fear our enmity more than our friendship and would be led thereby to seek our friendship." Which is what happened: but neither Eisenhower nor Dulles was capable of understanding this. After Stalin, much of the same thing. The records of the highly secret meetings of the Soviet Russian Politburo during the Hungarian Revolution of 1956 reflect that fear: Khrushchev and Co. were vaguely but deeply aware of Polish and Hungarian nationalism, while anxious to find and install the few reliable people they could imagine. That kind of worry and fear also explains their strange journey to elicit and assure the support of the Yugoslav Tito.*

---

*Brutality is often a reaction to some real or imagined injury and fear. In 1944 Hitler suddenly occupied Hungary—his ally and so-called satellite—knowing that some leaders in Hungary wished and had made a few uncertain attempts to detach their country from its fatal alliance with the German Reich. In 1956 it was Khrushchev and Soviet Russia that

A main characteristic of Hitler was hatred. True, he gained power in Germany partly because of his alliance with German conservatives, people who, after the 1918–1919 revolutions, were motivated by a fear of Communism. But he did not need these counterrevolutionaries for long; he discarded them with ease—since he was no counterrevolutionary but a true revolutionary of the radical Right. He declared hate, hate for the "enemies" of German nationalism both within and without Germany. This was a conscious, not an unconscious, element in his mind. As early as 1921 in one of his speeches he announced: "There is only defiance and hate [*Trotz und Hass*], hate and again hate!" And: "The lesson of life is to hate and to be hard." This impressed Goebbels when he met Hitler in 1926. Hitler kept telling him how he, Hitler, "had learned to hate." "His most beautiful phrase," Goebbels wrote in his diary, "yesterday: 'God has graced our struggle abundantly. God's most beautiful gift bestowed on us the hate of our enemies, whom we in turn hate from the bottom of our hearts.'" That was for him, and for many others, an element of strength. Compared to the power of Hitler's hatreds, even his love for the German people—the

---

did not allow Hungary to depart from the Soviet sphere. But there were profound differences in these brutal invasions. The Germans—and their local allies—were not fearful. The Russians, and their local allies, were. (Can anyone imagine Hitler flying at midnight to see Mussolini or Antonescu to seek support for a brutal decision that he had already made?— even when his Reich was besieged on all fronts by tremendous armies, while the Soviet Union in 1956 was not.)

living purpose of a national leader—amounted to less.* In this he was quite unlike Napoleon.

Even though hatred often results in physical inclinations and physical acts, it is essentially a matter of mind. (Again Hitler is a clear example of this. He was no sadist; he took no particular pleasure in watching, or even being informed about, the sufferings of his declared enemies.)

But while hatred amounts to a moral weakness, it can be, alas, often, and at least in the short run, a source of strength. Whence the advantage of the Right over the Left—especially in the age of democratic populism.

At or near the extremes of the political-ideological spectrum we may, then, observe these phenomena: the presence of fear among people of the radical Left, the presence of hatred among people of the radical Right. But such phenomena are not restricted to extremist believers in political ideologies. There exist fellow travelers on the Left but also on the Right: the latter are people whose fears are transmuted in the pleasurable feeling that they are now in the company of a league with nationalist haters. Yet these are tendencies, rather than categories. They are not simply attributable at-

---

*Bernanos: "In the spirit of revolt there is a principle of hatred or contempt for mankind. I'm afraid that the rebel will never be capable of bearing as much love for those he loves as he bears hatred for those he hates." (As true of elements of the Left as of the Right.)

tractions of particular ideas. They are human tendencies and therefore complex ones: inclinations and potentialities that are not fixed or predetermined. For men and women do not *have* ideas. They *choose* them.

Moreover, they have nothing to do with the so-called "subconscious," nothing with "A" or "B" types, or with "authoritarian" and "nonauthoritarian" personalities. Dualities in human nature are evident in a myriad of human attributes, beyond and beneath the duality of spirit and matter. So, too, neither fear nor hatred exists in its "pure" form. There is, almost always, a mixture of both. Khrushchev's fear in 1956 that the success of a Hungarian uprising would threaten the entire Soviet system was allied with his hatred of those who, to his mind, were ready to profit from it. Hitler's many expressions of contemptuous hatred for his opponents existed together with other, less frequent, expressions that he nonetheless felt compelled to utter: "I, for one, have never had an inferiority complex"—thus, within the heart and mind of this hate-ridden, willful, determined man we may detect at least a presence of fear. Within the minds of people who hate (and not merely dislike) Jews or Arabs, within the minds of others who hate Americans or capitalists, the element of fear is at least latent within their most rabid inclinations, evident in their exaggerated attributions of diabolical calculations and machinations of people whom they had chosen for their enemies.

It is insufficient and shortsighted to attribute such inclinations only to extremists. This is especially so during the devolution of liberal democracy into populism, popular nationalism being an inevitable ingredient of the latter, the wet cement that binds otherwise classless societies together. This, for instance, has now become the principal creed, as well as the principal asset, of "conservatives" and of the Republican Party in the United States, confident as they are in reaping large political and electoral* benefits from the "unpatriotic" and "liberal" characteristics of their potential opponents.[†]

Among other inclinations we ought to recognize, and without much difficulty, the accumulations of hatred (rather than of fear) among many people at spectacular sporting events. These are other examples of the coarsening of public behavior (or call it the militarization of sentiments).[‡] But

---

*Whence, too, the present fear by (2004) Democratic candidates lest they seem to oppose the war in Iraq too much.

[†]Thus immediately after the terrorist attack on New York and Washington (with which Iraq had nothing to do) President Bush and his advisers chose to provoke a war in Iraq well before the election of 2004, for the main purpose of being popular. This was something new in American history. There were presidents, from Polk through Lincoln to Wilson and Roosevelt who wanted war (and attempted to tempt their opponents "to maneuver [them] into firing the first shot") because of their belief that this was in the nation's interest; but *not* for the purpose of enhancing their popularity. (Not even Hitler chose war in 1939 to enhance or reaffirm his popularity with the German people, not at all.)

[‡]There are many examples of this: murders and even wars following international soccer matches in Central and South America; criminal hooliganism, at times debouching into murder, before, during, and after international contests in Europe; such behavior was practically nonexistent fifty years ago among American football fans, but no longer.

of course as Orwell or others remarked: children like to play at being soldiers, not pacifists. (As does too our present president.)

One last, and perhaps pertinent, generalization about the still prevailing differences between "Right" and "Left." Generally speaking, one hallmark of socialism and liberalism is the belief in the principal necessity of struggling against injustice. That is of course not an ignoble aspiration. Yet we ought to recognize not only the differences between Justice and Truth but their relationships to fears and hatreds. This is not the place to discuss their philosophical and metaphysical differences—perhaps save to remark that the sense of truth exists deeper than the sense of justice (and also that untruth is more poisonous than injustice). But it may be proper to cast a quick glance at the present historical condition of our world where injustices—social and racial and political injustices—are gradually eliminated or at least less frequent than ever before, while all over this world there hang enormous and depressing clouds of publicly propagated untruths. And the endless pursuit of justice that may lead, and indeed often leads, to the worst of human disasters. What is relevant here is that those who hate often believe that, apart from or beyond justice, they possess cer-

------

Here again notice the—at least temporary—prevalence of hatreds over fears: the desire to triumph or to crush one's opponents and some of their spectator supporters may be even stronger than the fear that one's team would lose.

tain truths about their enemies, important and decisive truths underlying the characters of the latter.

❦

The great Spanish thinker Miguel de Unamuno, in his *Tragic Sense of Life:* "Always it comes about that the beginning of wisdom is fear." Yes—because hatred can lead to knowledge but not to wisdom (and because within the depth of hatred there is also fear). And the hatred of others exists because it is natural for men to hate their own suffering: for what is vengeance but the wish to cause suffering in order to heal one's own suffering? Georges Bernanos understood this, profoundly. He saw that fear was underlying the politics and the statesmanship of the liberal democracies; but that it was also a founding element of dictatorships. He wrote in the 1930s: "Mankind is afraid of itself. . . . It is sacrificing its liberty to the fear it has of itself." "Hating ourselves is easier than we think," Bernanos also wrote. ("The real grace is to forget ourselves.") After the Second World War, he stated his great and dark prophecy of a future which could well be a new and unheard combination of hatreds and fears.*

---

*Here a footnote (not more than a footnote) to Christian readers who—against Darwin, and against all the theses of "science"—*ought to* believe that the coming of Christ to earth was the central event in the entire history of the universe. That involved the division among Jews (just

Beyond and beneath ideologies and politics, hatred and fear are easily detectable in the relations of races. These relations do not consist of perennial likes or dislikes. Fear dominant over hatred may turn to hatred dominating fear: into hatred combined with contempt, issuing from an instinctive recognition that members of another race or group have now became afraid of *them.*

In the relationship of the sexes the phenomena of hatred and fear are startlingly obvious. Women can hate as much as men do; but somehow active hatred is more common among men than among women. At one extreme, fear may enervate; at another, hatred activates. A woman may respect, or even admire, a man who hates, but not a man who fears; a man seldom admires a woman who hates, but he may respect a woman's fears. Hatred may lead to rape, while fear may lead to impotence. Both women and men have, on occasion, rape fantasies that may even titillate or fascinate them; but surely none have impotence fantasies that are titillating. This is a sad but inevitable element of the human condition: the attraction of evil in human hearts which is never purely physical but spiritual—the curse of the human condition, the ever-present condition of original sin. But there is a saving grace. (It is distinctly *not* a "grace under pressure.") Because all of the foregoing does not

---

as the end of the world, the Second Coming, may bring the great division among the remaining Christians). Those lawyers, judges, high priests who labored to condemn Christ were moved by hatred rather than by fear; Christ's apostles and followers by fear rather than by hatred.

suggest the inferiority of women—rather the contrary. It suggests—more, it is a mark of—their superiority, because of their natural inclination to the saving grace of love, not only latent but activated by their motherliness: because mothers, even more than fathers, love and protect those who fear.

In this respect the truth of Chesterton's aphorism must be instantly recognizable to anyone who knows something about the collective mass movements of our age. It is hate that unites people, whereas love is always individual, rather than collective. To this we may add what immediately negates whatever moral essence the purposes of class struggles or of racism or of modern nationalism may have: and this is that love is never the love of oneself, it is the love of *another*. That is the saving grace of mankind. Now much, very much depends on what will happen to women (and how they will regard themselves)—even more in the near than in the distant future.* Will they represent—more: will they incarnate—that saving grace?

History is unpredictable. It is full of examples where two apparent alternatives fade and are superseded by other matters.

---

*Can we expect too much from them—at least now? Consider but this symptom. "Gentleman"—today—is still a commendation: if a young punk or thug would hear someone saying that he acted like a gentleman, he would be stunned but not displeased; but no young woman—today— wants to be called a lady.

So far as politics and power go, most democracies are now fearful enough to reject extremes and their proponents (often at the cost of considerable legal legerdemain, but that is not the point). Fear and hatred are prevalent among us, manifest and evident in the increasing savagery—"savagery" is the proper word, not "violence"—in and around our everyday lives. Fear and hatred are human characteristics, and we shall never be able to eliminate them entirely. We must recognize not only their existence but their latent—and often more than latent—presence among those who wish to wield power. Whether some of them will be actually able to achieve power depends on many matters, most of them unpredictable, and seldom visible among the ever more complicated and manipulated appearances of politics and powers in this age of mass democracy. It depends whether and how the devolution of democracy into populism proceeds in the twenty-first century.

{TRIUMPH AND DISAPPEARANCE OF "LIBERALISM"}

A T THIS TIME, at the beginning of the twenty-first century and at the end of the Modern Age, is the test of democracy its avoidance of extremism, or even its immunity from it? There are many symptoms suggesting that, at least now, the popular appeal of extremes of Right (and of course of Left) are not strong. Will there be limits of the degeneration of democracy into populism? The political appeal of nationalist populism is not overwhelming, except here and there—less in western Europe than in the United States now.

But we must recognize a more fundamental phenomenon. This is the waning of liberal and parliamentary democracy. Here we face two, perhaps superficially contradictory, developments. One is that liberalism has, after all, triumphed: its self-imposed tasks are done. The other is the overall waning of its appeal, of the appeal it once may have had.

If "liberalism" means the extension of all kinds of liberties to all kinds of individuals, mostly as a consequence of the abolition of restrictions on all kinds of people, these have now been institutionalized and accomplished in formerly unexpected and even astonishing varieties of ways. (And with not a few fateful and, yes, deplorable consequences, such as laws approving abortions, mercy killing, cloning, sexual "freedoms," permissiveness, pornography . . . a list almost endless.) "Freedoms" of speech and of behavior . . . but then already more than one hundred and fifty years ago Kierkegaard put it right: "People hardly ever make use of the freedom which they have—for example, freedom of thought; instead, they demand freedom of speech as compensation." Many of these deplorable consequences were and are, again, results of the liberal emphasis on justice—if need be, at the expense of truth. But there they are. People throughout the world are now customers (I write "customers" rather than "beneficiaries," since many of those "benefices" are indeed questionable) of "freedoms" of which less than a century ago even the most radical liberals would not have dreamed.

At the same time, political and ideological liberalism has weakened, here and there even flickering out. One, but only one, evidence of this is the gradual disappearance of political parties calling themselves "liberal." Another is the decreasing number of people who designate themselves as "liberals." Another evidence is the decreasing interest and even practice of parliamentarism. In the United States for a long time now the main business of Congress has been conducted not on the floor but outside of it, in committees. Among other matters, the United States Congress has well-nigh abdicated its constitutional role of declaring wars. In Europe, both before and after World War II, there appeared disillusion, disinterest, even boredom with parliaments. (This is now largely so in Eastern Europe, after the temporary euphoria following the end of communism.) Yet another evidence is the widespread apathy about the European Parliament, a mechanism empty of authority and power. Elsewhere all that remains is the commerce of parliamentary votes sanctioning regulations or laws rather than creating new and necessary ones. Meanwhile, the protection of the rights of minorities (and of course of individuals) is almost entirely dependent on the publicity they and their advocates are able to produce—and thus gain support among the otherwise indifferent lawgivers.

The heyday of parliaments, of public opinion's acute interest in their debates, in their actual power, and in their liberalism occurred in western Europe about one hundred and fifty years ago. It had much to do with the structure and the function of what *was* "public opinion" then. It was reflected (as well often created) by the press. Like public opinion and popular sentiment, the "class" and "mass" newspapers were distinguishable; the former impressing themselves by their (often self-satisfied) "duty" to serve and to educate—and, at times, manipulate—"public opinion." A century and a half later only traces of that remain. Part of this is due to the gradual deterioration of democracy into populism. An even larger part is due to the, again gradual but well-nigh irreversible, acceptance of the purpose of even the remnant "class" newspapers to provide more and more entertainment. For populism is often crudely materialistic, dependent on the "bottom line" of financial accounting, accepting the standards of often very low common denominators in the very commerce of information and education. Here the function of television has been both overwhelming and deadening, since it is in the nature of that medium, and a consequence of the vast complexities and costs of its productions, to appeal to very low and most widespread common tastes (or, more precisely: what its producers calculate what those tastes are).

It is very unlikely that there will be anything like a return to the respect of parliaments. It is also unlikely that the extent of liberal permissiveness can go much further than it already has. (One telling example: the very cult of human nudity has bodily limits that are obvious and not merely "moral." But this does not mean that the pendulum will swing "back" [except perhaps a little, here and there].) Morals, fashions, history do not work like mechanical clocks; history furnishes ample demonstrations to the effect that while the Thesis-Antithesis-Synthesis formula may be logical, historical it is not.

One of the profoundest and most prophetic chapters of *Democracy in America* has Tocqueville's title: "Why Great Revolutions Will Become Rare." What he saw in America illuminated something for him that was contrary to what almost all conservatives in those times—indeed, almost all people who had their anxieties about the developing dangers to order—then feared: that the further development of democracy would bring about uncontrollable agitations and disorders due to the increasing participation of uncouth masses in politics. In sum, they feared revolutions, and perhaps unforeseeably frequent recurrences of them. To America Tocqueville came, saw, and illuminated something quite different. He recognized that in a democratic society and in a democratic age ideas (and beliefs, and convictions) will not succeed each other rapidly but, to the contrary, move slowly, sometimes with an agonizing lassitude of momentum. He also realized that this then-new development in the very gestation and composition of ideas also meant that the majority of people would not respond to extremes of radical agitation. Great revolutions will become rare, he wrote, because the new democratic societies tend to become materialistic, because more and more people will acquire possessions that they will not want to imperil; because eventually states and governments will tend to propitiate and ensure the welfare of the mass of their peoples through large bureaucracies—with the result that people become less free, though they may think that they are more so. This development, or devolution, into populist materialism Tocqueville regretted, while at the same time he saw, well-nigh alone among the best thinkers of his time, that Great Revolutions Will Become Rare. Which is what happened, with few exceptions, within the most developed democracies of the world.

There is reason to believe that—at least for some time— Great Revolutions will continue to be rare. There is some comfort in this condition. But also much has changed since Tocqueville's time. One development, which I contemplated earlier, is the weakening of the power, the prestige, the authority of states at the same time that their bureaucratic functions are still enormous. Probably much more important and fundamental is something else: the decline of healthy appetites for freedom at the very time when, together with other phenomena of licentiousness, an immense coarsening of civilized life has risen all around us. In this respect—illustrated by their behavior—there is hardly any difference between conservatives and liberals, or between self-designated Rightists and Leftists. Freedom, after all, is not merely emancipation, meaning the liberation or relaxation or absence of rules imposed on people by society, church, or state, by religion or government, by the tyranny of a ruler, by a minority, or by a majority. Freedom means the capacity to know something about oneself, and the consequent practice or at least the desire to live according to limits imposed on oneself rather than by external powers. This appetite for freedom is not extinct, not even in today's world; but the present "cultural" atmosphere provides something very different, indeed contrary to its proper nourishment.

In large parts of the world and even in the former Communist countries of Eastern Europe and in the Russias, the fear of police rule has waned (though it has not entirely disappeared), but there has been no real corresponding rise of liberalism. Meanwhile entertainment has pervaded, infiltrated, and more than often substituted for "information," as also television has by and large replaced the functions of a more or less "free" press. About these developments George

Orwell, in *Nineteen Eighty-four,* was quite wrong. He described a new kind of state and police tyranny, under which the freedom of speech has become a deadly danger, science and its applications have regressed, horses are again plowing untilled fields, food and even sex have become scarce and forbidden commodities: a new kind of totalitarian puritanism, in short. But the very opposite has been happening. The fields are plowed not by horses but by monstrous machines, and made artificially fertile through sometimes poisonous chemicals; supermarkets are awash with luxuries, oranges, chocolates; travel is hardly restricted while mass tourism desecrates and destroys more and more of the world; free speech is not at all endangered but means less and less. Much more important than the criticism of the prophesies of a once important book by an honest writer is the prospect of a modern democratic society in which the corruption of words and speech, in which television, with its near-monopoly on news and information, may be governed by the manipulators of popular majorities, in which opposition parties and papers are permitted to exist, but their impression and influence hardly matter since their voices are weak, and in which political freedom hardly amounts to more than to the absence of "totalitarianism" (a corrupt term, as we have seen). There are many countries in the world now where such a previously unimagined and unimaginable state of popular democracy has come to be.

All of this has a bearing on the history, on the present and future of "Right" and "Left." I have argued throughout this book that the old categories of "conservative" and "liberal" have become almost entirely outdated. "Right" and "Left": not quite so. But one tendency is evident. The "Left" has been losing its appeal, almost everywhere. It may be that in the future the true divisions will be not between Right and Left but between two kinds of Right:* between people on the Right whose binding belief is their contempt for Leftists, who hate liberals more than they love liberty, and others who love liberty more than they fear liberals; between nationalists and patriots; between those who believe that America's destiny is to rule the world and others who do not believe that; between those who trust technology and machines and others who trust tradition and old human decencies; between those who support "development" and others who wish to protect the conservation of land—in sum, between those who do not question Progress and others who do.

"Man prefers peace, and even death, to freedom of choice in the knowledge of good and evil," said Dostoevsky's Grand Inquisitor. Fine words, and applicable to many historic conditions (to wit, to the majority of the German people under Hitler), but still to be taken with more than a grain of salt (because this great unkempt Russian prophet's convictions of freedom were rather peculiar, due

---

*As indeed in 1940, at that most critical moment of Western civilization when Hitler almost won his war, when all over the Western world the crucial divisions were there within the Right, between Churchill and his Conservative opponents, between De Gaulle and Pétain, etc.

to the strange Russian orthodoxy of his religion. Less reso-
nant but more telling for us may be the words of his contemporary Lord Salisbury: "Free institutions, carried beyond the point which the culture of the nation justifies,
cease to produce freedom. There is the freedom that makes
every man free; and there is the freedom, so-called, which
makes every man the slave of the majority." It was in the
beginning of the fake-revolutionary 1960s that the fine
American Catholic theologian John Courtney Murray wrote:
"Perhaps one day the noble many-storeyed mansion of democracy will be dismantled, leveled to the dimensions of a
flat majoritarianism, which is no mansion but a barn, perhaps even a tool-shed in which the weapons of tyranny may
be forged." After all, history has plenty of examples when
tyranny came to be preferred to anarchy or even to anything
approximating anarchy; that there are conditions and situations when large masses of people prefer the relative physical security of police rule, even if stringent. This brings us
to a last gloomy consideration, which is the rise and the
prospect of criminality.

{THE RISE OF CRIMINALITY}

ALL OVER THE WORLD, but especially in what are called "the advanced," modern, democratic nations, criminality has been rising, steeply, during the past half-century. Its evidence is all around us. What this means for the welfare state: the need for more prisons, etc., needs no illustration. More disturbing is another development within our increasingly fluid societies. This is the enormous increase of what may be called amateur, rather than professional, criminality. Less than a century ago many professional (and therefore habitual) criminals were known by the police. There has never been a precise division between criminals and the rest of the civic population; yet even though the lines of distinction were fluctuating, they were somehow recognizable. This distinction has now largely disappeared. What has happened is the very appeal of certain acts of criminality, and the consequent prestige of successful amateur criminals, especially among young people. Worse: what has emerged is the shocking disappearance of social disapproval, let alone ostracism, of many criminals—and especially of so-called white-collar criminals—whose eventual condemnation by the courts many people regard as, well, bad luck.

Now there exist neighborhoods, and also ethnic groups, where the successful criminal—again, especially among the young of both sexes—has the appeal of a hero. Of course the prestige of physical bravery, of daring, even of occasional brutality, with their visible and palpable ability to inculcate fear among their potential opponents, has always existed (and now this appeal is also enhanced by films, television, and other forms of "entertainment"). But I must draw attention to something that appeared during modern dictatorships. This is the overall—and not only occasional, and often inevitable—dependence of police regimes on criminals. During the Third Reich, and particularly within its most dreadful prison and extermination camps, SS personnel became more and more dependent on criminals (and especially on criminals capable of brutality) among the imprisoned population—e.g., the so-called Kapos. In the Soviet Gulags, too, this practice was widespread and went even deeper than what had taken place in Auschwitz, etc. In these Russian camps the criminals often became even more powerful (while they were more numerous) than the official guard personnel. What this meant, among other things, was something remarkable and frightening to which few, if any, students of so-called "totalitarianism" paid any attention. This was the ascendancy of raw power over ideology. At first sight it seems that Auschwitz or the Gulag were horrid examples of an official ideology stretching into extreme practices, perpetrated by their most committed and fanatical minions. Yet, especially during the last years of the Third Reich, the SS was willing, openly and without scruples, to collaborate with all kinds of criminals. It was less and less committed to its official ideology or even to German nationalism; its contempt for its victims bound it together with its collaborating criminals. This contempt was something else than hatred; it was inhuman rather than human (for hatred is human, after all); it was inspired by a confidence in brutal power. This was even more so in the prison camps of the Soviet Union, where it was certainly not Communist ideology that inspired the guards and their criminal allies. (One—indirect, but nonetheless observable—result of this phenomenon was the tremendous wave of all kinds of criminality immediately during and after the collapse of the Soviet Union, leading—ten years later—to a confrontation between some [but only some] of the criminal nabobs and moguls and the attempt by Putin, a former secret police official, to reestablish a new kind of state police authority.)*

In our democracies: will the weakening of the authority of the state lead to further and further increases of criminality? Will people, everywhere, become more and more

---

*That democratic governments are not exempt to the temptation to use criminals for their purposes is obvious. In 1943 the Mafia was supported in Sicily by Americans; Roosevelt depended on Italian-American mafiosi to secure the operation of docks in New York and Brooklyn. Examples of the CIA hiring criminals and of its dependence on them (including druglords) are too numerous to mention.

dependent on their protection by all kinds of well-paid police personnel? Will entire societies divide in ways that are already happening in teenage classrooms: between those who are (or at least seem) strong and those who fear them? These are not rhetorical questions; but we cannot tell. What we can tell is something inherent in populism, which is that within its innate contempt for its opponents and outsiders there is that ever-present compound of hatreds and fears.

Great Revolutions may indeed Become Rare. But so will, too, privacy, security, lawful order, family.

{A NEW, PROFOUND, DIVISION}

WHEN TOCQUEVILLE wrote that Great Revolutions Will Become Rare, he meant political revolutions, as we also do. But the application of the word "revolution" to politics is not much more than three hundred years old. We have also seen that the political employment of the adjectives "conservative" and "liberal" are less than two hundred years old, and largely so are the political designations of Right and Left. What we now must consider is whether at the end of the so-called Modern Age, at the time of the universal acceptance of the principle of popular sovereignty, new divisions may occur, or are already occurring.

The most important new condition (which Tocqueville did not and could not foresee) is the rampant technology—perhaps more precisely: the extreme mechanization—of the world. It is a consequence of this that, for the first time since Adam and Eve, it has become possible for mankind to destroy itself, or at least large portions of the earth. Until now, the great physical catastrophes—earthquakes, epidemics—*all* came from the outside. No longer. There is, as yet, not much active or sufficiently widespread contemporary anxiety about such a prospect. The vast majority of men and women (and, in many places of the world, at least understandably so) are still looking forward to "Progress." There exist, however, a few signs both on the surface of events (that is, even in politics), and many more below that surface, that indicate or at least suggest that an uneasiness with, and sometimes even a conscious and active opposition to, the still-present idea of "progress" have begun to appear, especially within the so-called "advanced" states and nations.

The first signs of this appeared on the political surface in the 1960s, in Germany. It was the formation of a "Green" party, composed mostly of young people, opposed to further industrialization and mechanization, dedicated to protecting nature, the "environment." Sooner or later Greens began to appear in other countries, too. However, nowhere have they won more than small percentages of the popular vote; in many countries where mechanization and the actual as well as potential destruction of nature were prevalent, the numbers of the Greens were even less significant. Again we may confront an inconsistent duality. The Greens— and this is their weakness both in the short and in the long run—are prone to much of the same kind of schizophrenia, split-mindedness, that is now characteristic of both "liberals" and "conservatives." About the protection and the defense of Nature the Greens are traditionalists. About the protection and the defense of traditional human institutions and moral standards they are not. They are often vocal proponents of abortions, "free" love, "free" speech, etc., contemptuous of marriage, family, permanence, etc. In sum— and this goes well beyond the ideology of the Greens— many of the "environmentalists" (a bad word, to start with)* are also antihumanists.

Yet the Greens are only a superficial symptom of something deeper, perhaps the foam on the top of a slowly rising and moving tide. More and more people, including many who are hardly aware of the Greens, have now become uneasy with mechanization, automobilization, impermanence: consciously or not, with the once modern (and now quite antiquated) idea of "Progress." Thus there are reasons to believe that the great divisions in the future will be between

---

*"Environment": something outside of us. Yet we are participants in Nature, which exists both inside and outside of us.

those who have begun to oppose or at least rethink the still extant concept of "Progress" and those who have not. Yet because of the lamentable, and often fatal, slowness of the movement of ideas and of their public propagation, because of the encumbered and sclerotic character of democratic and bureaucratic institutions, much time will pass until such a rising tide of sentiments and opinions, no matter how widespread, will appear on the surface and have definite political consequences.* A vast, and manmade physical catastrophe or epidemic may have to occur before a coagulation or crystallization of such a development, leading to great changes, involving, among other things, the very vocabulary of politics.

But this writer is a historian, not a prophet. Let me, therefore, attempt to draw some attention to matters that have already happened. The old, Darwinist antithesis of Science

---

*The Italian poet Eugenio Montale circa 1960: "In the age of science and technology reason is towed along behind, and every effort is made to pension it off." José Ortega y Gasset circa 1950: "Civilizations have perished . . . [only] from petrification or arteriosclerosis of their beliefs." Tocqueville one hundred and sixty-five years ago: "We live at a time that has witnessed the most rapid changes of opinion in the minds of men; nevertheless it may be that the leading opinions of society will before long be more settled than they have been for several centuries in our history. . . . It is believed by some that modern society will be always changing. . . . For myself, I fear that it will ultimately be too invariably fixed in the same institutions, the same prejudices, . . . that mankind will be stopped and circumscribed; that the mind will swing backwards and forwards forever without begetting fresh ideas; that man will waste his strength in bootless and solitary trifling, and, though in continual motion, that humanity will cease to advance."

and Religion has already passed; it is behind us. (So is the once scientific distinction between what is "organic" and what is "mechanical"—though not enough people know this.) Opposition to ever increasing and ever more drastic and inhuman applications of "Science" is no longer merely "conservative" or "reactionary" or "traditionalist" or even "religious." Our contemporary, the American farmer, thinker, and writer Wendell Berry, wrote in 1999 that the great next division of mankind may be "between people who wish to live as creatures and people who wish to live as machines." And Søren Kierkegaard one hundred and sixty years ago: "Summa summarum. The human race ceased to fear God. Then came its punishment; it began to fear itself, began to cultivate the fantastic,* and now it trembles before this creature of its own imagination."

Consider the corruption of speech, evident in the thoughtless use of a still-present political vocabulary. "Conservatives" in many countries but, alas, especially in the United States, are the vocal votaries and propagators of technology, of mechanical "progress," of global "corporate capitalism," often at the cost of nature and of its resources, against the protection and preservation of that permanence

*Consider only the American popular (and puerile) interest in Monsters, Robots, Space Aliens, and perhaps, too, a popular president, Ronald Reagan, who thought and spoke in terms of the fight of Good and Evil according to *Star Wars*. And perhaps also the no less ominous names now given to American aircraft: Black Hawks, Warthogs, Predators, Raptors.

of residence which is the fundament of civilization. (They often claim in public that they are defenders of family values, but only when such an assertion seems to be popular.) "Liberal," in the English language, was once the very antithesis of "mechanical," but that was very long ago. Since then the "liberal" belief in "progress," with many of its destructive consequences, has gone on largely unquestioned. And because of the liberal espousal of questionable "freedoms" (mercy killing, enforced early "sex education," the sanctification and legalization of homosexual "marriages," unrestricted immigration of large masses of people, etc.), antiliberalism may remain more popular than anticonservatism, perhaps especially in the United States. But this goes both beyond and beneath politics, as it involves deeper inclinations of belief.

{IDEAS AND BELIEFS}

THROUGHOUT THIS LITTLE BOOK I have tried to draw attention to the importance of ideas—but only inasmuch as these ideas represent conscious thinking; about how they rise and arrive, how they move, how they invade thinking—for let me repeat: people do not *have* ideas but *choose* them. This is a difficult subject, for at least two reasons. One is philosophical (more precisely: epistemological): there is an overlap between ideas, faiths, beliefs. This has always been so, and there is no sense to delve into their distinct philosophic definitions. The other difficulty is that we must consider how the older, nearly perennial difference between what people believe and what they think and say has now become even more complicated because of a democratic and populist phenomenon: the difference between what people think they believe and what they really believe.

There exists now a dormant, and perhaps even nascent, appetite for faith—for some kind of faith, for faiths of all sorts—at the time of the decline of the sense of "enlightenment," at the end of what, exaggeratedly and often falsely, was called an Age of Reason. At the same time there is the evident and rapid decline of the prestige and the influence of churches, at least in the West. The decreasing proportion of people who are churchgoers and the rapid fall in the numbers of men and women wishing and willing to become priests, pastors, nuns are but superficial symptoms of this decline. (It may change: for these are consequences, not causes.) Meanwhile, liberalism and social democracy have, almost inevitably, altered Protestantism, with its reminder of sin first diminishing, then evaporating. But, as in so many other phenomena of political life, here and there a radical and nationalist populism (one example: Northern Ireland) has merged with the reappearing remnants of a fundamentalist Protestantism (example: the United States), a kind of near-fanatical spirituality which, however—because of its shallowness and individual permissiveness—is ephemeral. Among the Eastern, Greek and Russian, Orthodox churches of eastern Europe the nationalist and populist characters of the different national churches remain largely what they have been for almost one thousand years.

That was, and remains, the consequence of what we may call Constantinism (since it began with Constantine the Great): the willingness of churches, and of their peoples, to accept and even to venerate and worship (and on occasion even sanctify) the authority of monarchs, dictators, imperial rulers, when these invite their churches to assist them at their maintenance of law and order.

What has been happening with the Roman Catholic Church and with its believers is more complex. Two hundred years ago—we may even mark its lowest point in two thousand years: 1799—the prestige and the power of the papacy seemed to vanish altogether. This did not happen. There were—perhaps short-lived but nonetheless extant—Catholic spiritual and intellectual revivals during the past two hundred years, as well as resurgent evidences of the power and of the influence of certain popes (note but the nonmeasurable but nonetheless obvious contribution of the present pope to the piecemeal collapse of Communism in Poland, not more than twenty or twenty-five years ago). During the nineteenth and the early twentieth century there were popes and committed Catholic thinkers who declared that Catholicism and Liberalism and Democracy were incompatible. As far as democracy was concerned Tocqueville was among the first who did not think so; he saw the, sometimes surprisingly durable, coexistence of Catholicism and democracy in the United States (and also in Ireland). He also saw—and was deeply vexed by—the reappearance of Constantinism (he did not use that term) in his own France in and after 1848, when the church supported the dictatorship of Louis Napoleon because of the fear of revolutions and of socialism, for the sake of maintaining law and order. Still, there have been enough inspiring examples of the Roman Catholic Church rejecting Constantinisms and dictatorships, especially when rulers had thought themselves to be sufficiently powerful to oppose and even attack the church, as in the case of Henry VIII of England, when not only saints such as Thomas More but at least some of the clergy were "not inclined to the fashion of the world as it goeth now."

However: here too we must recognize a deep, perhaps tectonic, shift. By the twentieth century the great danger to and temptation of the church and its people was no longer Constantinism but populism. This is not the place to illustrate or even to enumerate the manifold evidence of Catholic nationalism and populism in many countries, and perhaps most tellingly in the Germany of the Third Reich,* and then in the United States. It may be appropriate to draw attention to symptoms of the devolution during the past decades. The sudden melting away of the number of priests and nuns and religious aspirants in the 1960s may have been the result of clergy and of religious "inclined to the fashion of the world as it goeth now"—perhaps the mainspring of the pedophiliac and homosexual scandals of priests that were revealed recently. These were results of the permissive secularized lives of the clergy, perhaps less because of the reforms of Vatican II than because of the sexual and social climate of the 1960s (and after). But what has been the reac-

---

*One example: Bishop (later Cardinal) von Galen, after regretting that the National Socialist government prohibited a religious pilgrimage in Münster in 1935: "But we are Germans and would regard a rejection of the state as insidious treachery against the *Heimat* and *Volkstum* to which we belong and serve with our hearts. . . . Rejection of the state would be a sin against God who has created us as Germans." Note this commingling of populist nationalism with Constantinism. (But then this was the same von Galen who in a single famous sermon in 1941 both condemned Nazi euthanasia and praised the German invasion of the Soviet Union.)

tion of the people of the church to these lamentable revelations? Criticism—often warranted, sometimes not—of cardinals and bishops; but, more than often, propagation to include more and more of the laity in the governance of the church, as if that were something long overdue, democratic and healthy. No one thought that the American "laity," ever so often, has been more "conservative" than "liberal," more nationalist than supranationalist, not more but less spiritual than some of the older priests and hierarchs. When in 2003 Pope John Paul and the Vatican clearly and directly spoke against the American Republicans' war against Iraq (also against the American humiliation of the dictator after his capture), the great majority of American Catholics were unaware, unknowing, uninterested, or, at best, indifferent to that. The record of the Catholic Church in Germany during the Third Reich was neither clear nor unsullied, though it was better than that of most other churches. But: had the German Catholic "laity" become included in the governance of the German Catholic Church in 1933 or after, the record of that church during those harrowing years would have been infinitely worse.

We may yet see a decline in the acceptance of the monarchical and hierarchical powers and prestige of the church not unsimilar to what happened fifteen hundred years ago—when, for example, in 499 in Rome two rival bishops were elected by rival groups of the clergy and the people, and when appeals were made to the near-barbaric ruler (Theodoric) to choose which one of the bishops should be installed. And we may yet see the contrary, the Catholic Church being the last, embattled and tattered but, still, here and there visible—bastion and inspiration of personal integrity, decency and, yes, of liberty and of hope.

{HOPE, AGAINST FEAR}

HATRED MAY BE STRONGER than fear. But not deeper. And not preferable to it. Jesus said to his followers: "Do not fear." (Only recently the present pope has kept and kept repeating, insisting on this.) Hatred and fear, Right and Left: these are not only modern phenomena. Consider what happened two thousand years ago. "Opinion" was then, too, "the queen of the world." Then, too, "the people" mattered. On Palm Sunday, five days before Jesus' crucifixion, the people in Jerusalem sang his praises and cheered him as he ambled through the streets in their midst on a plain donkey. Less than five days later: "Crucify him!" Fear of him and hatred of him, a deadly combination, moved the corrupt high priests and lawyers who wanted him out of the way, better dead than red. The aristocratic representative of the imperial monarchy, Pontius Pilate, was doubtful. (Even more so was his wife.) Here was, again (as often in the twentieth century), a difference between two Rights, between the skeptical upholder of law and order, the gentleman Pilate, and the fanatic and cynical spokesman of his narrow interests, Caiaphas. But "the Left" were not uniform either. By Friday the people had turned against Jesus. They feared rather than hated him. Many of the women in Jerusalem knew that. They (and the patrician Joseph of Arimathea) came to weep and to bury him. And—not immediately but very soon—their hope rose and came into the world, stronger and more lasting than were their fears.

But this was two thousand years ago (and yet not to be contemplated only by Christian believers). So let me then speak of that important condition (or call it "factor") which is the historicity of hope. Yes, there is that kind of hope that Christians must have: hope in the future because of God's forgiveness, in their hopeful redemption from sufferings, physical and moral. But there exists, too, a secular and historical condition of mankind. This is the forever condition that evil does not proceed indefinitely in this world. Or, in other words: honesty may not be always the "best," meaning the most practical, policy; but dishonesty ends up always as the worst, the least practical policy and behavior. Good words (and good poetry) survive because bad words (and bad poetry) do not. Contemplate Kierkegaard's profound and yet commonsense truth: "It is possible to be *both* good and bad, but it is impossible *at one and the same time* to become both good and bad." The choice is ours, because of human free will, which exists whether people believe in it or not. And this recognition is especially timely now when, together with the devolution of democracy, we are already in the midst of an increasing intellectualization of everyday life, of the increasing intrusion of mind into matter, with all of its—unforeseeable—consequences, when the causes of the worst of catastrophes may no longer be outward but inward, arising from the inside of mankind.*

Therefore I feel compelled to conclude this little book with a different tone than heretofore. The music of this small and surely imprecise jeremiad was tattered and somber; but let me dissolve these dark tonal harmonies with a melancholy but perhaps surprisingly soothing (though by no means angelic) chord. To appear as a hopeless pessimist, a prophet of ever closer darkness, accords neither with my temperament nor with my historical understanding. I know that the signs of a new barbarism are all around us, but I not only will not but cannot—honestly—predict that this will inevitably overwhelm us. I remind myself of what Burke once said: "He

---

*Luke 6:43: "The good man brings good things, out of the good stored up in his heart, and the evil man brings evil things out of the evil stored up in his heart." Mark 7:21: "From within, out of man's hearts, come evil, through its immorality, theft, murder, adultery, greed, slander, arrogance, and folly. All these evils come from inside . . . "

that accuses all mankind of corruption ought to remember that he is sure to convict only one." Like Tocqueville, I do not know why God chose to have mankind enter the democratic age; but, whatever the brummagem sources and corruptions of democratic or even populist intentions, their results are, more than often, unforeseeable and not equivocal. Deep within Tocqueville's mind resided this latent question: do men's institutions change their characters, or is it, rather, the other way around? Hitler and Stalin are gone, and George W. Bush will soon be gone, too; but then so are their German National Socialism and their Communism and so will be his "conservatism." Consider another example, during the sordid 1960s: the civil rights legislation applied to the American South, promoted by all kinds of people, yes, good as well as bad, and out of the most varied human motives (like the Civil War). Yet this second change, involving the traditional political and social structure of the South, was accomplished with little bloodshed and no revolutionary turmoil. At the same time one of its consequences was the almost entire loss of the once traditional and local Democratic South to Republicans, many of who have translated themselves to the South from the North (a new generation of carpetbaggers, one might say). Nor did the final and legal emancipation of blacks in the South lead to an increasing harmony of the two races, whether in the American South or elsewhere. It led to great shifts in the relations of whites and blacks but not to a disappearance of fears and hatreds, the end of which is not yet. Still no one, not even the Republican political carpetbaggers in the South, wishes to see, let alone say, a reconstruction of the old inequalities. That is but one example of the complexity and of the unpredictability of history, and of the unforeseeable consequences of the still evolving, and devolving democratic age.

Index